ALAN BARNARD is Emeritus Professor of the Anthropology of Southern Africa in the University of Edinburgh. He studied in the United States, Canada and England and has taught at the University of Cape Town, University College London and the University of Edinburgh. Since 1974, he has conducted field research with Bushmen or San in Botswana, Namibia and South Africa. He served as an Honorary Consul of Namibia for eleven years, and in 2010 he was elected a Fellow of the British Academy. Among his many books are *Research Practices in the Study of Kinship* (co-authored, 1984), *A Nharo Wordlist with Notes on Grammar* (1985), *Hunters and Herders of Southern Africa: A Comparative Ethnography of the Khoisan Peoples* (1992), *Kalahari Bushmen* (children's book, 1993), *History and Theory in Anthropology* (2000), *Social Anthropology* (2006), *Anthropology and the Bushman* (2007), *Social Anthropology and Human Origins* (2011), *Genesis of Symbolic Thought* (2012), *Language in Prehistory* (2016) and *Bushmen: Kalahari Hunter-Gatherers and Their Descendants* (2019). His works were all written in English, but have been translated into 18 other languages.

HUNTERS AND GATHERERS

WHAT CAN WE LEARN FROM THEM

ALAN BARNARD

Emeritus Professor of the Anthropology of Southern Africa
University of Edinburgh

Hearing
Others'
Voices

BALESTIER PRESS
LONDON · SINGAPORE

Balestier Press
Centurion House, London TW18 4AX
www.balestier.com

Hunters and Gatherers: What can we learn from them?
Copyright © Alan Barnard, 2020

First published by Balestier Press in 2020

A CIP catalogue record for this book
is available from the British Library.

ISBN 978 1 911221 69 2

Photo credits: Cover: !Xoõ woman and her child.
All illustrations are by Alan Barnard, except no. 6 which is
by Jerome Lewis, no. 16 by Joy Barnard, and nos. 4, 7, 12, 14
and 17, which are from Wikipedia.

Contents

Foreword

by Thomas Wildlok

Today, hunting is often considered to be a privilege, a privilege of high social class and of high expenses—and at the cost of the animals involved. Gathering is often considered to be a sign of poverty, of having neither fields nor domesticated animals and, in the modern urban setting, maybe as relying on dumpster-diving and on scavenging deposit bottles for a living. The hunter-gatherers introduced by Alan Barnard in this book are very different.

These are not societies of class and rank since they typically put an emphasis on equality and mutuality when hunting—also in their relation to the animals they hunt. They are described as living in relative affluence because they can rely on what they gather and on what the environment shares with them. Moreover, the groups of people that anthropologists for short label 'hunter-gatherers' are of great interest for much more than their hunting and gathering practices alone.

For the largest part of human history living by hunting and gathering has been associated with a number of other social and cultural features that many people today find very attractive and rightly begin to appreciate. A life full of creativity in terms of music, art and ritual. A life with a high degree of personal autonomy, of great importance attached to social relations between humans but also with the non-human world. The life of those labelled 'hunter-gatherers' therefore fascinates many of us today for a number of good reasons. The fascination is greatest among those anthropologists, like Alan Barnard, who have lived many years with hunter-gatherers and who have made it a profession trying to understand them.

This book is important because it is easy to be mistaken about hunter-gatherers. Our own ideas of what it means to hunt and to gather easily come into the way.

The book spells out the great human achievements that have been brought about by humans who hunt and gather—across the millennia. But it also shows that these achievements go beyond hunting and gathering alone. They depend on particular ways of understanding the human environment and the world at large.

Barnard points out that there is a lot to be learned for our own lives when getting to know a life based on hunting and gathering. This also has to do with the fact that their mode of living in many ways continues to be deeply enshrined in what we are and what we do. At the same time, learning from hunter-gatherers helps to unsettle us in a positive way. Maybe your and my way of doing things is not without alternative after all. And getting to know alternative ways of life that have been successfully put into practice by the people described in this book are a better start than fantasy and science fiction.

However, the biggest lesson of all is to understand how things are connected and how people are connected. This also means that it would be naive to think that one could simply import isolated practices from elsewhere without there being effects that reach far into all domains of life.

The living hunter-gatherers that Alan Barnard introduces us to in this book are often prevented to continue their way of life because of what the rest of us do: the amount of resources that we use and waste, the grabbing of land that serves a world economy banking on unsustainable growth, the power that we abuse when dealing with indigenous minorities and a false sense of superiority towards hunter-gatherers.

Ironically, what may help us most in this situation is something that is part of the inheritance from our hunter-gatherer past and that we can learn (again) from the hunter-gatherers described here: a curiosity towards what is new to us, paired with a sense of appreciation about what allows us to live on this planet as humans.

Thomas Widlok
Professor of the Cultural Anthropology of Africa
University of Cologne, Germany

Preface

When I was in my early twenties I was given the chance of a lifetime. I had studied anthropology, but all of a sudden my book-learning was turned on its head. I found myself in the Kalahari Desert and living with a small band of real hunters and gatherers. They knew nothing of telephones (mobile or otherwise), but they did know how to live off the land. I was, at last, able to acquire a real education.

Today 'we' are used to having sophisticated technology. And when I say 'we', I mean those of us who can read. Thousands of years ago, our ancestors didn't have computers or telephones. These are very recent inventions, and it is too easy for us to forget this. Nor did they have any form of writing. Instead, they told stories. They learned about the environment and how to live in it by just doing it. Older people showed younger ones how to make tools and how to hunt, how to gather wild foods and where to find them, how to eat and what to eat.

Our ancestors once lived entirely as hunter-gatherers, and they lived in this way for millennia. 'We' have forgotten a great deal of our collective learning, and in this book I hope to reintroduce a little of it. I am grateful to Ruth Finnegan, the series editor, for pointing this out and for asking me to put these thoughts into words. The book is intended mainly for the young, but in truth I think we can all learn from hunters and gatherers.

Alan Barnard

1.

INTRODUCTION:
WE ARE ALL HUNTERS AND GATHERERS?

We are all hunters and gatherers. Humankind has lived on this planet for around 315,000 years, and for nearly all of this time we have been hunters and gatherers. The date of 315,000 years was only arrived at very recently, in the year 2017 to be precise. Even if we accept the traditional date of 200,000 years ago, this is still a very long time. And for nearly all this time, roughly 96 per cent of it, we humans lived solely by hunting and gathering. There is no way we can go back to living as hunter-gatherers, but to understand ourselves it helps to know that this is where we came from.

Before we turn to modern hunter-gatherers, let's begin with a brief look at human evolution. But let's be careful! All humans alive today are modern humans. Even those who live in deserts and jungles do so with a knowledge that most people do not. They have chosen their way of life, just as we have chosen ours. We should, I think, be careful about judging them for their choice. Rather, they have a great deal we can learn from: living in peace, living without government, enjoying life with few possessions. Also, *not* working too hard, but living off the land. As we shall learn later, hunter-gatherers do *less* work than people who have agriculture. These are all attributes of modern hunter-gatherer society, and that is why we can learn from hunters and gatherers.

A brief note on human evolution

Whether it was 315,000 years ago or 200,000, there is no doubt that humans evolved in Africa. The specific site referred to in the key paper was in Morocco. However, this doesn't mean that humans evolved only there. Rather, human evolution happened right across Africa. It is important to remember that we are talking here about 'modern humans', the species known as *Homo sapiens*. Other species, such as australopithecines and Neanderthals, did exist earlier. The dates for those begin around 3,500,000 years ago for australopithecines and 400,000 years ago for Neanderthals. The earliest *Homo* was in between, about 2,400,000 years ago. If this is already seeming complicated, don't worry. Anthropologists (those who study such things) are still working out the details, and things are rapidly changing. Table 1 will give you an idea of the current state of thinking on human evolution. A word of caution though! Much of this is speculation. We do not really know when early humans invented symbolism or first communicated, or even their communication was through gesture or through speech. All the dates here are given in BP (before present).

Table 1. Human evolution: current thinking

2,600,000 BP	First stone tools (among australopithecines)
2,400,000 BP	Appearance of the genus *Homo* (*Homo habilis*)
1,800,000 BP	Controlled use of fire (by *Homo ergaster*)
1,200,000 BP	The FOXP2 mutation, which made language possible
600,000 BP	True hunting and gathering (as opposed to scavenging)
400,000-300,000 BP	Use of wooden spears
315,000 BP	Earliest Homo sapiens (in Morocco)
270,000 or 170,000 BP	Possible use of ochre (in Zambia)
200,000 BP	Traditional date for earliest *Homo sapiens*
160,000 BP	Use of red ochre and earliest fishing
100,000 BP	Origin of grammar and full language
100,000 BP	Earliest mythology
74,000 BP	Eruption of Toba volcano and population bottleneck

70,000-60,000 BP	*Homo sapiens* migration from Africa to Asia
60,000 or 48,000 BP	Habitation of Australia
50,000 BP	Traditional date for emergence of language
42,000 BP	Very early music
	(the 'Neanderthal flute') (in Slovenia)
35,000 or 20,000 BP	Habitation of the Americas
25,000 BP	Cave painting
25,000 BP	Neanderthals die out
12,000 BP to present	Modern hunter-gatherers and cultivators

For nearly all of our time on earth, we 'anatomically modern humans' lived solely by gathering wild plants and hunting wild animals. Before modern humans, hominins (or human-like creatures) were alive. These proto-humans included australopithecines, who evolved in southern and eastern Africa. They lived by hunting and gathering too and also by scavenging. In other words, by scavenging bits and pieces from animals killed by other creatures: hyenas, wolves and so on. Scavenging was more common among early humans or human-like creatures than among later ones, and humans gradually learned to improve early hunting techniques. We have learned this through evidence from archaeology, which is a discipline closely related to anthropology.

The transition from living mainly by scavenging to

hunting and gathering is believed to have occurred around 600,000 years ago. By that time our ancestors had already learned to light fires and to use them for warmth and for cooking. Debates rage over when language began. Experts tell us that the genetic change that made language possible (known as the Forkhead box protein P2, or in short FOXP2) occurred around 1,200,000 BP. Mice have the same gene, but obviously they haven't invented language! (In mice, the gene regulates breathing and thinking.)

I will just single out one important date, 74,000 BP. This is the assumed date of the explosion of Toba. Toba was once a volcano but now a lake in modern Indonesia. It is important in prehistory because of what happened afterwards: the population of the earth was reduced to as few as 2,000 people. This is because of the 'volcanic winter' that followed. There simply was not enough food to support the population that lived through it. Later, the species *Homo sapiens* was able to leave Africa and to migrate across the globe. But we are talking about very small numbers. Pre-*Homo sapiens* creatures (such as 'Peking Man' and 'Java Man') had left Africa before, but they died out long before this. Others, such as the Denisovans, did survive in very small numbers, and a few did contribute to the human gene pool. In other words, we are descended from them too!

Estimates of the first *Homo sapiens* group to leave Africa are as small as 150. That's right: possibly just 150 people. By 48,000 years later their descendants were able to reach Australia and beyond. Some say the migration that first reached Australia was about 60,000 years ago, and some anthropologists think the date was even earlier.

Modern humans almost certainly got to Australia before we got to Europe, although a tiny number (the Denisovans) were in Europe already. This is the opposite of what many people think, but it is true. The dates assume known sea level changes and the fact that the only way to get to Australia would have been across a stretch of water. In other words, the first Australians arrived by raft or maybe a small boat. As for the Denisovans, they were a pre-modern people only discovered very recently. The evidence is entirely genetic, from a finger bone found in Siberia in 2010.

Getting to the Americas was easier than getting to Australia. In ancient times there was a land bridge across the Bering Strait that connected Russia to North America. Migrants (all hunter-gatherers) could have walked across. This would have been as long ago as 35,000 years ago. It is difficult to know. Some experts say it was even 50,000 years ago, but for purposes of Table 1, I have assumed the more likely date of 35,000 years ago. Later the first

Americans would learn to cultivate crops, independently of the origins of agriculture in other parts of the world. Other continents would come to be settled later, still by hunter-gatherers, and eventually almost the whole world would come to grow crops.

A final word

In 1968 the anthropologist Richard Lee and the primatologist (a person who studies apes and monkeys) Irven DeVore wrote these words: 'We cannot avoid the suspicion that many of us were led to live and work among the hunters because of a feeling that the human condition was likely to be more clearly drawn here than among other kinds of societies.'

In this famous quotation we have the essence of what it is to be a hunter-gatherer, or what it is to study them. Lee and DeVore were looking for a clue about the human condition. In the frontispiece of their book *Man the Hunter* they noted that in 10,000 CE the world's population was 10 million. (CE means 'of the Common Era', the date now shared among most all peoples. So 10,000 CE is the same as 10,000 BC, or about 12,000 BP or 'before present'.). All of these people were hunter-gatherers. In 1500 CE the world's population was 350,000,000. 3,500,000 (or 1 per cent) were hunter-gatherers. But by 1900 CE the world's population was 3 billion. Only 30,000 (or 0.001 per cent) were hunter-gatherers. One may quibble with the exact figures, but the gist is very clear. 'Natural humanity' had virtually ceased to exist. The word's remaining hunter-gatherers are all we have left of natural humanity. Yet we must always remember that they are fully *cultural* too. They have just as much culture as any other people. It is just directed differently from what we in the West are used to.

Summary

To sum up, what I am suggesting is that to be a hunter-gatherer is to be human. Humans lived as hunter-gatherers for more than 300,000 years, and as keepers of livestock and cultivators for only 12,000 years. Virtually no-one lives purely by hunting and gathering today. Why study hunter-gatherers? Because to understand them is to understand ourselves and human nature.

2.

THE LABEL 'HUNTERS AND GATHERERS'

The label is accurate, but perhaps deceiving. For a start, most of the food they eat is gathered, not hunted. Even though, for example, the Bushmen of the Kalahari eat more meat than 'the inhabitants of Texas' (as one anthropologist has put it), most of what they eat is vegetables. That's where Bushmen (or San, as some call them) get their calories.

Only very rarely do hunter-gatherers today live mainly by hunting, although humans once did live that way. Hunter-gatherers often have little in the way of vegetables, since their environments these days are so poor. Neanderthals did live mainly by hunting: we know this from archaeology. Neanderthals ate very big animals, such as mastodons, a kind of extinct elephant that once roamed across Asia and North America. The Neanderthals encountered mastodons in parts of Asia and killed them and ate them. Of course, killing one was no doubt a little difficult! The Eskimo or Inuit are about the only example of people today who still live mainly by hunting. In the very brief time I spent in the Arctic, in eastern Greenland, the hunters there were living mainly off of seal meat.

The traditional label

The traditional label has long been 'hunters and gatherers' or 'hunter-gatherers'. The classic anthropological text was called *Man the Hunter*, which may be worse! This all may sound very sexist, and probably it is. Men invariably do the hunting, and women do the gathering. Usually, gathering is done by two or more women together. Hunting can be done either alone or in a group. The label 'gatherer-hunters' has been suggested too, but that hasn't really caught on. Some Western anthropologists prefer the term 'foragers', but that doesn't work in several countries. For example, in Japan or in Spanish-speaking countries, where 'foraging' is something only animals do. To say otherwise is problematic. 'Hunter-collectors' sort of works (or *chasseurs-cuilleurs* in French), but this is not the usual English phrase. In French, *chasseurs-cuilleurs* is the typical expression. Gatherers, collectors, foragers. What is your personal preference? And why? This is possibly a useful point to debate. There is no easy solution to the problem of what to call them. In this book, let's just call them hunters and gatherers or hunter-gatherers.

I have just mentioned a few languages. The choice is not that odd. Japan is today a major centre of hunter-gatherer studies. There are a small number of hunter-gatherers on Japan's northern island, Hokkaido. But that is not the reason. The reason for Japan's important place in hunter-gatherer studies has to do more with the fact that Japanese people were once forbidden to travel abroad. This was after World War II. Japanese anthropologists turned their attention to studying, instead of people, a kind of monkey called the macaque. The idea was that this gave them an insight into humanity. When later they were allowed to travel, they became experts on chimpanzees. And later still, human hunter-gatherers, specifically Bushman groups in southern Africa. A few also went on to study herders or pastoralists, such as the Turkana of Kenya.

As for Spanish-speaking countries, much of South America is inhabited by people who live in small communities. Most of these people are *not* hunter-gatherers, but cultivators of sorghum and manioc or cassava. However, they do share some features of social organization with hunter-gatherers. They live is tiny units and often don't have chiefs. But because they are cultivators, they do have to work harder to harvest their crops of root vegetables (manioc) and grain (sorghum). Contrary to popular belief, hunter-gatherers spend *less* time working (hunting and gathering) than herders or cultivators. This is because they value their free time rather than the goods they accumulate.

French-speaking countries are important in hunter-gatherer studies too, for the obvious reason that many hunter-gatherers, the 'Pygmies', live in the former French colonies of central Africa. The Baka of Cameroon and Gabon and the Mbuti of the Democratic Republic of Congo are famous examples. Commonly, Pygmies themselves speak French, as well as their African languages such as Baka and Mbuti, and of course this has made life easy for French-speaking anthropologists. So the anthropologists have gravitated to where the hunter-gatherers are.

My own background is in social anthropology. This discipline emerged in the UK during the nineteenth century. In the US there is a very close relative, called cultural anthropology. These are basically the same thing. Whatever we call it, social or cultural anthropology is part of a constellation of anthropological fields. Others are archaeology, biological anthropology and anthropological linguistics. I said earlier that humans evolved in Africa. We now know this, but for a long time anthropologists thought that humans had evolved in Asia. This was the prevalent idea in the nineteenth century (although Charles Darwin thought otherwise), when Europeans were just coming to grips with the idea of evolution. Europeans then were *also* just coming to grips with Africa! Advances in many sciences in the twentieth century taught us a great deal. Through genetics, among other sciences, we can today be fairly confident in what we know. Within anthropology itself, we have learned a good deal, and the results have been quite starling.

For example, how can we live without government? Would violence not break out everywhere? Is violence not the natural behaviour for humans?

Well, no! The answers are usually found in reading political philosophy, but I wonder if in fact anthropology offers just as good a solution? In this book we shall explore questions like this one. There are any number of peaceful societies in the world. In general these peaceful societies are very small-scale ones, and very often they are the societies of hunters and gatherers. We shall explore these issues later in the book.

Hunter-gatherers and early humans

Let us return to early humans. At first, I resisted the topic of *early humans* because I was afraid it might give the wrong impression. Modern hunter-gatherers are thoroughly modern. There is nothing 'early' about them. Nevertheless, some reflection on the idea of living by hunting and gathering alone is worthwhile. It is not the way we live today, but it is the way our ancestors lived.

Could you live that way? I certainly couldn't. My career has been spent living *with* hunter-gatherers, but their ingenuity and resourcefulness puts my book knowledge to shame. Living as a hunter-gatherer is very difficult, except for people brought up to live that way. I have mentioned evolution, and I have already mentioned one kind of early human: the Neanderthals. In fact, the Neanderthals spent longer on earth than Homo sapiens, our own species. Some anthropologists argue that Neanderthals *were* part of our own species. They distinguish *Homo sapiens neanderthalensis* from *Homo sapiens sapiens*. Neanderthals were 'wise' too (that's what *sapiens* means), but perhaps just not quite as 'wise' as we are. Neanderthals had, on average, brains as big as ours or bigger! They walked upright, and the consensus is that they had language too. Presumably, they hunted in groups: think about hunting a mastodon as an individual! And by language, I mean real language and not just grunts and screams. They may have sounded different because their speech organs were different from ours. They were larger than us, because they were adapted to a cold climate. Otherwise, they were nearly the same as we are.

Figure 1 shows the duration of *Homo sapiens* and of Neanderthals. As we see, they spent longer on earth than we have. They died out, but we are still here. And don't forget: for most of our 315,000 years we humans have been hunter-gatherers. Only for the most recent period, about 13,000 years at most, have we had crops to grow. The date for the first livestock is about the same or a little earlier. So we were all hunter-gatherers once, then became cultivators and herders of livestock. But humanity evolved at different rates, and the very small number that still hunt and gather are just those who retain a simpler human existence.

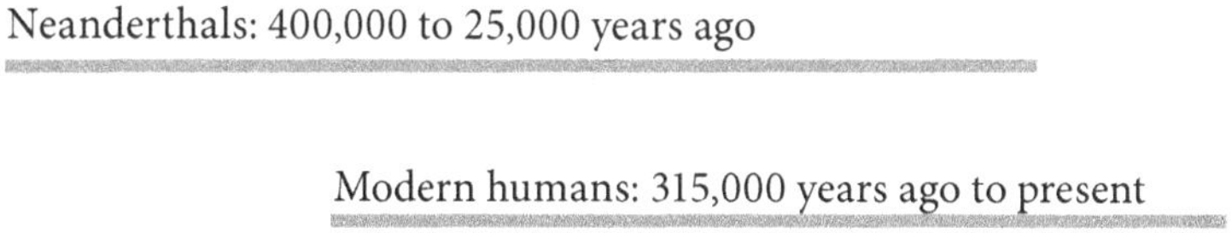

Neanderthals: 400,000 to 25,000 years ago

Modern humans: 315,000 years ago to present

Figure 1. Neanderthals and modern humans: duration of time on earth

Nomadic or territorial?

Actually, nomadic and territorial are not opposites. Nor can we say that hunter-gatherers are precisely one or the other.

Let me explain. There is indeed a widespread belief that hunter-gatherers are *nomadic*. However, their 'nomadism' is pretty much always within their own territories. Their territories are usually well defined. This is shown in the diagrams in Figures 2 and 3.

Figure 2 is based on the settlement pattern of the Ju/'hoan-si of the Kalahari Desert. The Ju/'hoan-si are exactly the same as the !Kung: their name has now been changed to reflect the preference of the Ju/'hoan-si themselves. The hyphen is optional, and the *–si* just makes the word plural. The Ju/'hoan-si come together

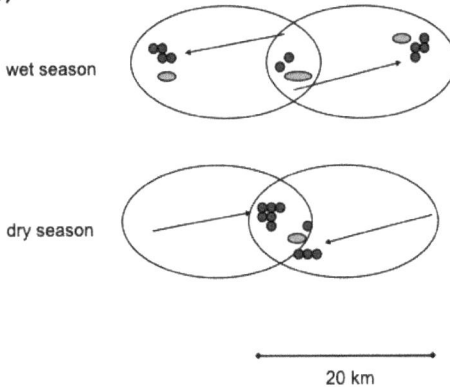

Figure 2. The settlement pattern of the Ju/'hoan-si

(or *aggregate*) in the dry season because they can! They use waterholes that are dotted about their land. In these diagrams, each tiny circle indicates a family, and the ovals represent the waterholes. The larger circles represent band territories. As we see, for the Ju/'hoan-si in the dry season, more than one band can share the same waterhole. But as shall see in Figure 3, the Ju/'hoan settlement pattern, in fact, is only one of those that Bushmen practise. (Ju/'hoan is the singular form, or the one used for adjectives.)

Figure 3 represents an entirely different settlement pattern, that of the G/ui or G/wi Bushmen. The / and !

G/ui

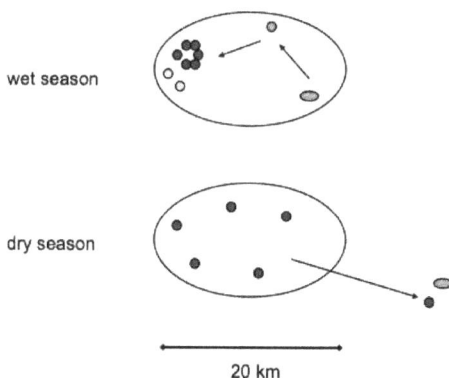

Figure 3. The settlement pattern of the G/ui

symbols, by the way, represent 'clicks'. These along with some other 'clicks' are found in several of the languages of southern Africa. From front to back of the mouth, the ones found in Bushman languages are written ⊙, /, ≠, //, !. Some of you may also know the clicks found in, for example Zulu or Xhosa (Nelson Mandela's language). These are c, x and q. (The c represents /, x represents //, and q is !. The sounds are the same, just a different spelling system.) The Ju/'hoan-si and the G/ui speak very different languages. They are both groups of 'Bushmen', but they have spent tens of thousands of years learning their different local environments. Each group has had to cope with different constraints, and through such a long time apart each group has developed its own language. Although the seasons are the same, the resources are different. The distance between the two groups is about 300 kilometres or 186 miles.

Have a close look, and compare the two diagrams. In a way, they are opposites. The Ju/'hoan-si come together, more than one band at a time, in the dry season. The G/ui separate (or disperse) in their dry season. This pattern was studied by anthropologist George Silberbauer in the 1960s, about the same time that Richard Lee was studying the settlement pattern of the Ju/'hoan-si. In the Ju/'hoan case, two bands are illustrated, and in the G/ui case just one. Each ethnic group will have several bands, each numbering about 20 or 30 people.

In the wet season, the G/ui band in the diagram move as a group from waterhole to waterhole. When the water holes dry up, the group will live off of the *tsama* melons. These are wild melons and are full of water. They provide all the water the G/ui need late in the wet season. In the dry season, there will be no *tsamas* left. There are no sources of water at all in that part of the Kalahari, so each family will go its own way. When water becomes really scarce, one or more families can move outside their territory to find water. In the Ju/'hoan case, two bands share a waterhole. In the G/ui case, one family is shown leaving its territory to find water in the dry season, bottom right.

What studies of these groups tell us is that *small differences* in the local environment can make *big differences* in how people use the land. Both groups know their environments very well, and their choice of settlement pattern reflects the best use of their resources. The Ju/'hoan-si and the G/ui live in different parts of the Kalahari. The wet and dry seasons are the same, but the patterns of settlement are very different. Ju/'hoan-si come together at waterholes in groups of families during the dry season. Ju/'hoan-si have a number of waterholes, but the G/ui don't. The *band* is the main unit of social life for all Bushmen, but as we see different Bushman groups have to use their environments quite differently.

I first drew theses diagram in the 1970s, before the Internet or PowerPoint. The diagrams were, of course, schematic, but I think it works best this way to show the use of territory. So are hunter-gatherers territorial? I leave it to you to decide, but in my view they both *are* and *are not*. Partly it is a matter of definition.

What have we learned so far?

Actually, we have probably learned quite a bit. There is no really correct term for hunter-gatherers. Although Neanderthals were hunter-gatherers, they are very different from modern hunter-gatherers. We don't know the details of Neanderthal settlement patterns, but we do know that modern hunter-gatherers have very sophisticated ways of dealing with their scarce resources. The fact that the Ju/'hoan-si and the G/ui are so different shows this. Each group has learned how to cope. Far from being primitive, they are thoroughly modern in their attitudes to things like water, food and seasonal migration. In a way, each group is territorial, but *territoriality* is in the eye of the beholder.

3.

COULD YOU LIVE AS A HUNTER-GATHERER?

We know that our ancestors were hunters and gatherers, but what about you? Could you live in this way? Can you hunt? Can you gather wild foods? What kind of 'wild foods'? Think about it: your ancestors certainly did this, but could you?

The first humans lived in a time long ago, and they possessed spoken languages long before anyone had writing. Have a look at Tables 2 and 3. How would you do as a hunter-gatherer? The exercise is not as easy as you might think. For instance, hunter-gatherers don't have to think much about planning ahead. But they do need to think about where they can find food. They have grown up spending their lives learning this. We in the West are used to things like going to the supermarket. We also live in a time of computers, credit cards and mobile phones. We don't have to catch, collect or forage for our food and bring it home. We just have to pay for it!

Table 2. Hunting and gathering versus herding livestock

	HUNTING and GATHERING	HERDING LIVESTOCK
water	Fewer worries about water	Concern over water
environment	Knowledge of the environment	Knowledge of herding skills
food	Search for wild food	Search for grazing for livestock
possessions	Lack of possessions	Chance to acquire possessions
free time	Free time	Long working hours
meat sharing	Sharing meat	Trading meat as well as sharing meat
land and people	Need for individual space	Need of space for migration
planning	Lack of planning	Long-term planning needed

Table 3. Hunting and gathering versus cultivating

	HUNTING and GATHERING	CULTIVATION
water	Fewer worries about water	Concern over water
environment	Knowledge of the environment	Knowledge of cultivation
food	Search for wild food	Planting and picking food
possessions	Lack of possessions	Chance to acquire possessions
free time	Free time	Long working hours
sharing and trade	Sharing possessions	Trading
land and people	Need for individual space	Need of space for crops
planning	Lack of planning	Long-term planning needed

We see that learning the skills needed to herd animals is quite similar to learning how to cultivate. Hunting and gathering are easy, and herding livestock is in many ways more difficult. So, how easy are any of these? Which way of life is better, or healthier? In 1976 a team from Harvard University and elsewhere investigated. This is what they found:

> The authors correct the widely held view that so-called primitive societies are basically aggressive, territorial, and possessive or that life in the state of nature is nasty, brutish, and short. They describe, for example, how the !Kung work shorter hours and eat more protein than members of many more advanced societies. There is a conspicuous absence of the clinical signs of heart disease, and blood cholesterol levels are about half those in Western society and among the lowest ever recorded for a human population.

The !Kung, by the way, are the same as the Ju/'hoan-si, just another name for this famous Bushman group.

There is a lot of material in this short quote! Are 'primitive' peoples really so primitive? In his book *Leviathan*, in 1651, the English philosopher Thomas Hobbes wrote about primitive peoples. He said they lived a way of life that was 'nasty, brutish and short'. He didn't think of them as living is *societies* at all; he thought that they lived *before society* was invented. We now know that this is not the case. Adam Smith's approach helps here. He probably didn't know the details, but his understanding of society was economic, whereas Hobbes's was political.

In a lecture written about 1762 Smith talks about an imaginary society of around thirty or forty families, about 140 or 150 people altogether. People lived 'by the chase', in other words by hunting. This was the first stage of what was eventually called 'four stage theory'. The other stages were the age of shepherds, the age of agriculture and the age of commerce. We know today that gathering is usually more important than hunting, even in 'the age of hunters'. Still, as Lee and DeVore suggest, hunter-gatherers show

Photo 1. Bushman hunter with his bow

few signs of heart disease. Also, they work fewer hours than people do in 'advanced' societies.

Two words describe the !Kung or Ju/'hoan-si: 'Bushmen' and 'San'. *Bushman* is the traditional word. *San* is actually slightly older, dating from the seventeenth century, but which is better? This is a difficult one. The word 'Bushman' has been criticized for being demeaning and even sexist. The word 'San', on the other hand, was described by one nineteenth-century writer, Theophilus Hahn, as meaning 'vagabond and rascal'. Presumably, San were 'vagabonds' because they kept moving. They were 'rascals' because they stole other people's cattle. We now know that Ju/'hoan-si is better than !Kung because it is the preferred term of Ju/'hoan-si themselves. Perhaps this is a point worthy of debate.

The fact is that outsiders have long had to bear demeaning remarks and overtly grudging insults. This, of course, does not make *them* worse people. Rather, it is a symptom of our own society's understanding that *we* see *them* in such a way. It is due as much as anything else to the fact that they are poor, even if poor by choice. As another nineteenth-century writer, the missionary John Philip, commented (perhaps ironically), 'John the Baptist was a Bushman!' The reason why San or Bushmen *stole other people's* cattle was for food. As for John the Baptist, it was his deliberately meagre lifestyle that made him a bit *like a Bushman.*

Material culture

Anthropologists talk a lot about material culture. This just means the things that a group has. In the case of hunter-gatherers, there is little in this regard: bows and arrows, digging sticks, cooking pots, stuff to make shelters, clothing and that's about it. The lack of material culture makes it easy for people to travel. Living as they do, in bands, means that having few possessions can be very useful. However, hunter-gatherers do have *some* sophisticated technology. Building huts (usually done mainly by women) can involve some tricky skills, and of course in the Arctic building igloos is also a skilled job.

The photo here shows a dry season camp, with a man playing his favourite possession, a *segaba*. It is a one-stringed musical instrument, a bit like an upside-down fiddle. It is not originally a Bushman instrument but borrowed from the Tswana. They are a cattle herding and cultivating people who live near the Bushmen. We can see how sparse the material culture is. Note too that this even applies to the simple hut, which has no roof. It is really just a screen to break the wind.

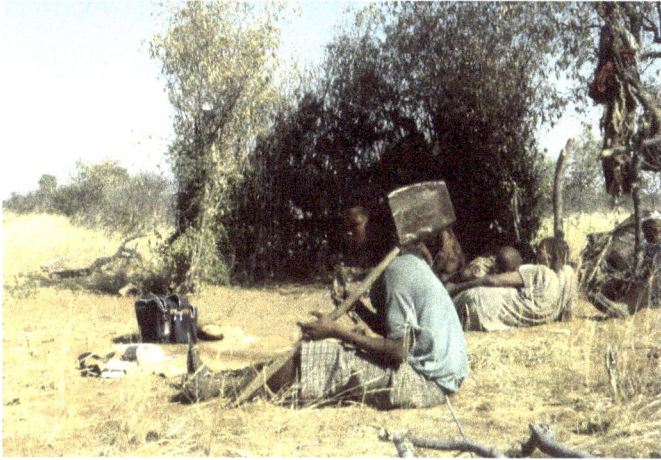

Photo 2. A dry season camp with a man playing the *segaba*

Herding and cultivating

Who has an *advanced* society? What would the important criteria for definition be? As for the importance of herding and cultivation, most archaeologists agree: *herding wild animals probably came first*. Yet it may not be that simple. Following reindeer around and occasionally killing one? Is that reindeer-herding?

What about cultivation? Sewing a few seeds, or managing what grows naturally? How do you define *cultivation*? However you define it, cultivation too is a little problematic. For example, in the Torres Straits (between Australia and Papua New Guinea), what we call 'cultivation' began simply as the management of what grows wild. Is this truly cultivation?

Crops like wheat and oats were first grown deliberately in the Middle East. The ancestral equivalents were very much like the wild varieties. They only became like the modern ones later. It is the same in the Americas, where wild varieties of corn or maize were gradually developed into the crops we know today. Partly, this is because of selective breeding: choosing what grows and produces best. Then concentrating on cultivating these. That is how cultivation began.

Whichever came first, there is no doubt that herding and cultivating both take up more hours than hunting and gathering. Hunter-gatherers spend *so little time* hunting and gathering because they know how to do these things efficiently. So, Hobbes was wrong about this. Hunter-gatherers don't live lives that are 'nasty, brutish and short'. Their lives can be just as nice, just as fulfilling, as our own. They are just different, and partly this is because their attitudes to work are so different. Defining what we mean by 'work' can be difficult. However we define it, herders and cultivators do more of it than hunter-gatherers. Hunters and gatherers do less work than we do, but they do not accumulate wealth. They would rather do less work. Richard Lee estimated that Ju/'hoan-si spend only about two or three hours a day in work-related activities (hunting, gathering, making arrows and digging sticks, building huts and so on).

A short note on language

Hunter-gatherers spend a lot of time talking! Jerome Lewis, an anthropologist who studies with Mbendjele Pygmies in central Africa, notes that it is common for several people to speak at the same time. We think it is polite to speak, just one person at a time. They have no problem when people speak across one another. On the other hand, they don't worry about silence. They can sit near each other completely silent, for hours at a time! You might think that this is stupid, or that it means that *they* are stupid. In fact, nothing could be further from the truth. When to speak and when to be silent are cultural. What works in one culture may not work in another.

When I began my own fieldwork in southern Africa, I had to learn to communicate. This meant learning a difficult language. The language is called Naro. Naro and many other Bushman languages are not easy because they have difficult grammars. They have difficult vocabularies too.

It also meant in a sense to learn how to think a bit like a Bushman! I have kept up with Bushman studies ever since, but I'm still not very good at Naro even though I have spoken it for many years. It has thousands of words, and possibly the most complicated pronoun system in the world. One linguist tells me there are 86 pronouns in the Naro language! Actually, these are technically PGN markers (person – gender – number). Another Bushman language, /Xam, has at least 32 verbal prefixes and suffixes, and for nouns, at least 14 ways to form a plural! These are *hunter-gatherers*, and they have very simple technology. So why do they need such complicated grammars?

Remember that hunters and gatherers live in very small groups. So, with an average group size of 20 or 30, why do you need 86 pronouns or 14 ways to make a plural? And as if this is not enough, some Bushman languages like Ju/'hoan, !Xoõ and !Xun have very, very complicated systems of meaningful sounds. The numbers are ridiculous: !Xun (spoken in Namibia) has 141 phonemes, as they are called: the sounds that make up words. In comparison, English gets away with considerably fewer. Depending on which *kind of* English, around 44. Again, why? And Bushmen generally will know not just their own language, but also the languages of surrounding groups too. I have known Bushmen who can speak nearly a dozen different languages.

So, who is brighter: a literate Briton or an illiterate, but multilingual, !Xun? Or a silent Mbendjele?

4.

BAND SOCIETIES

Politically, hunter-gatherers are known as band societies. What this means is that they are structured in terms of 'bands'. In Aboriginal Australia bands were once known as 'hordes', although this term has fallen out of use. Each band may consist of 20 or 30 people, or over 100. In either case, this is assumed to be about the right size for people to get to know each other. Of course bands may beak up, with individuals going their separate ways. We have seen this, for example, among the G/ui Bushmen, where in the dry season bands break up into family units. Often though, bands break up permanently. This happens sometimes when there are disagreements within a band.

In modern anthropology, the term 'band' was made promoted especially by American scholar Julian Steward. He famously studied the Shoshone Indians of California. However, Steward was mistaken about the typical makeup of band societies. He distinguished two types: *patrilineal band societies* and *composite band societies*. 'Patrilineal' just means related in the male line, fathers and their children. 'Composite' band societies are bigger, with more than 100 people in a band. However, we now know that patrilineal band societies rarely exist. Composite band societies do exist, especially in the Canadian Subarctic. There they seem natural, and people like the big gatherings.

The reason Steward believed in patrilineal bands was that he thought it was normal for people to stick with their fathers. He also imagined a kind of *matrilineal* band society, where people stuck with their mothers instead. We now know that both these ideas are fallacious. In fact, people can get together under *either* parent. This is what Bushmen do. Other peoples do much the same: central African Pygmies, the Batek of Malaysia and so on. Even Australian Aborigines don't worry much about organizing themselves particularly around males or females. Remember, Steward was writing in the 1930s. His book about this was only published in 1955. People had very different attitudes to gender back then. Even when groups tend to form on a patrilineal basis, this can be as much by coincidence as by plan.

A few years later another towering figure of hunter-gatherer studies came along. This was Elman Service. Basically, he agreed with Steward in nearly every respect. The only major change was that he called patrilineal bands *patrilocal*. This just meant that people lived in the *same place* as their fathers. In truth, the name change didn't matter much. Band societies tend to be *bilateral*. This means that it does not matter whether one sticks with the father or with the mother. Either side of the family is fine! But neither Steward nor Service were just being sexist. They simply did not realize the difference between an *ideal pattern*, what everyone assumed was true, and the one which is real. Hunter-gatherers may have described to their anthropologists the ideal, but a closer look would show that the reality is different.

Photo 3. Band on the move

What does it mean to live in a band society?

Among hunters and gatherers, the band is the main unit of social organization. Sometimes smaller units are found too. These are often called task groups. They get together for *tasks*, such as hunting or gathering. Usually men do the hunting, and women do the gathering of wild plants. For example, a group of women may get together to gather roots or fetch firewood. These are often collective ventures, each group going out together either for safety or just for enjoyment. The band is the main unit, but ethnic groups often have a larger identity as members of what is sometimes called a *band cluster* or a *tribe*. A band cluster is just a group of related bands, and a tribe is a group who speak the same language.

Band societies in general share several attributes. For a start, they need a large area for the size of their population. This is because hunter-gatherers need more land than other peoples. Hunting and gathering may not require much effort, but hunter-gatherers do need lots of land. Another attribute is the lack of hierarchy. Some say that they are anarchists. They don't like bosses! They enjoy their freedom, and this means freedom to roam where they choose. Flexibility is another hallmark. It follows that they don't, in general, have chiefs, but there are exceptions!

The *potlatch*

I mentioned that chiefs are rare. The most famous *exceptions* though are the groups in the Northwest Coast of North America: the Haida, the Tlingit, the Kwakwaka'wakw (formerly called the Kwakiutl) and so on. These groups practise the *potlatch* ceremony. This is basically one in which chiefs compete to give more and more of their property away. In the past, especially in the late nineteenth century, they *destroyed* their wealth. The most common

Photo 4. A *potlatch* ceremony
Watercolour by James Gilchrist Swan (1818–1900).
Wikipedia, 'potlatch', accessed 1 December 2019

commodity for destruction was a stack of blankets. They did this by burning them! To give is great, but to burn is even better! That was their view. In British Columbia and later in the United States, the governments had to stop this peculiar practice. Even one late nineteenth-century expert called it 'a worse than useless custom'. But why should the people of British Columbia, Washington State and Oregon do such a thing?

The answer lies in their notion of prestige. In this, these hunter-gatherers are almost unlike any others. Most hunter-gatherers value equality. The Northwest Coast peoples instead value the ability to put down other people. They don't just give things away: they do so in a way to make themselves look better than their neighbours. They used to throw big feasts. That would allow them to gain prestige.

The peoples who practise the *potlatch* live in an area that is very rich in resources, and these resources are spread unevenly. The chief resource is *fish*, specifically wild salmon. So if this year my patch is full of salmon, I can gain prestige by caching lots of them and giving them away. Yet a mechanism for doing this is necessary. Imagine I am a chief. The mechanism is that everyone in my group brings fish to me, as their chief, and I redistribute them! If next year another group had more fish, they would do the same. You could say that things evened out over time, although in a way this misses the point. The peoples of the Northwest Coast simply don't behave like 'normal' hunter-gatherers. They have their own way of solving the problem of too many fish in one place, and not enough in another.

The *potlatch* still exists, but is form has been changing. Today, it is often more like a wedding feast. Yes there is competition in this, but it is regarded as a bit more 'normal'.

The typical band society

Don't be put off by all the definitions. Basically, flexibility and freedom are what are important to almost all hunter-gatherers. Typically, the attributes of band societies then are these:

- large territory for the size of population
- lack of social hierarchy
- flexibility and freedom
- no state, no chiefs (with a few exceptions)
- no war of all against all
- universal kinship

We will take up *universal kinship* in detail later, but for now remember that everyone in a band is related.

Universal kinship is just the means to extend this idea throughout the whole of a society. Everyone within one's own society, then, is regarded as 'kin' whether we know the exact relationship or not.

Living in a band society is a good way to live. Obviously there are difficulties, but things like drought and not having enough food are rare. It is herders who tend to have these difficulties. Hunter-gatherers sacrifice the accumulation of property for a way of life that is care-free. However, it does require people to live in small groups and with a lot of land. So there are good things about living in a band society, and there are bad things. Hunter-gatherers have been around for far longer than other people. They have gradually *adapted* to living as they do. Perhaps the *potlatch* is simply an unusual form of adaptation?

The size of a band depends on a great many things, and the scope for change tends to work for hunter-gatherers. Flexibility and freedom are, for them, everything.

5.

SHARING AND GIVING

Sharing is one of the most important things that hunter-gatherers do. Yet they don't share just because they are being kind. They share because it benefits their societies. Society works because of it. In a way then, sharing itself is an adaptation. It helps hunters and gatherers cope with the fact that their environments have scarce resources. It enables them to make a living both in bad times and in good times.

Let me give one famous example of sharing: what is called *xaro* or *hxaro* among the Ju/'hoan-si. The *x* is pronounced as a breathy sound, a little like an *h* but harsher. The spelling *hxaro* is very common, but in truth it is not quite correct. So let's use the correct version. *Xaro* was discovered in the 1970s by economic anthropologist and archaeologist Polly Wiessner. Recently she has decided to drop the *h*. Here is how *xaro* works. Suppose I have a nice hat, for example, and you don't have a hat. You might say: '*Xaro* me your hat.' I can either give it to you, or refuse. If I give you the hat, then the two of us become *xaro* partners, and a day, a month or a year later I can ask you for something in the same way. It may be an exaggeration to put it this way, but the practice seems to bind together the whole of society because and it serves to equalize the distribution of property.

Every Ju/'hoan person will have a number of *xaro* partners. Importantly, only material possessions can be *xaro*-ed. Other things can be given too, but not in *xaro*. To take another example, meat sharing is common in many Bushmen groups, but there are complicated rules about this. The owner of the arrow that killed an animal is the owner of the meat. But this is *not* the person who shot the arrow, because people lend their arrows to other people. Not every Bushman group knows about *xaro*, but for those ones that do it seems to work. The sharing of meat is very common, and of course this is a good thing too. The animal killed may be very large, and sharing it means that everyone gets a taste.

Another common exchange item among hunter-gatherers is fish. There rules about how these are exchanged too. We have already seen the example in the *potlatch* in the Northwest Coast of North America. Fish, specifically salmon, go to the chief, and he redistributes them to other groups. The extreme variability or the resource here assures that everyone gets some. They just have to give their catch to the chief, so that he can redistribute it. In general, hunter-gatherers share more than we in the West do. That is because we have different values. The values work for them, but would they work for us?

Figure 4 illustrates the importance of sharing in hunter-gatherer ideology.

Hunter-gatherer ideology
(Sharing is valued)

sharing of food	appropriate social behaviour
accumulation of food	anti-social and selfish

Western ideology
(Accumulation is valued)

storing food and property	appropriate social behaviour
immediate consumption of food	anti-social and selfish

Figure 4. The value of sharing

Territory and the sharing economy

Let's go back a step. We humans had no agriculture and no crops until only about ten or twelve thousand years ago. So for at least 95 per cent of our time on earth, we human beings have been pure hunter-gatherers (or scavenger-hunter-gatherers). That is the way humans have been designed to live, by hunting wild beasts and by collecting wild plants. Other things, like reading, writing and computers, only came much, much later. So what can we learn from hunters and gatherers? A great deal! Not only is the practice of hunting and gathering the natural lifestyle of all humanity; it is also an effective, ecologically and a sound way of making a living. The typical hunter-gatherer spends *less time*, not more time, in work-related activities than the average farmer or the average livestock herder. Her nutrition is better. And he avoids the diseases associated with stress and over-work.

In a sense then, being a hunter-gatherer is *good for you*. This doesn't mean that we can all be hunter-gatherers though. In evolutionary terms we can't. There simply isn't room on the planet for all of us to enjoy this way of life. One thing that hunter-gatherers do *need* is space to pursue such a lifestyle. With a growing population on earth, that kind of space simply does not exist. Sharing food and sharing other things, such as rights to hunt on each other's land, are ways around this problem.

Hunter-gatherers value free time more than they value wealth. This ideology encourages sharing. Typically, hunter-gatherers have evolved social mechanisms that encourage sharing and discourage accumulation. To accumulate is seen as bad, while to share, particularly meat, is encouraged. This theme is intriguing in that it has marked a return to classical interests in hunter -gatherers as an economic, as opposed to a political, category. Other recent themes emphasize the ecological foundation of hunter-gatherers and hunter-gatherer studies. These classic interests seem set to continue through the twenty-first century. This is in spite of the fact that the hunter-gatherer way of life has been reduced over the past ten or twelve millennia. Hunter-gatherers may represent the most long-standing subsistence strategy the world has ever seen! It is a most theoretically challenging one, but *not* of course one that is at all common in the world today.

Photo 5. Two boys by the fire

I once lived in the Kalahari Desert of Botswana, Namibia and South Africa. Namibia is in fact the least populous country in Africa and second-least populous on earth. Only Mongolia has a lower population density. The Kalahari is bigger than France and covers about 900,000 square kilometres or 350,000 square miles. The population density of Botswana is about one person per 3 square kilometres or one person per 9 square miles, but this includes vast areas where Bushmen are only a small minority. Sadly, hunter-gatherers need that kind of space.

The idea of sharing may be related: hunter-gatherers share with others because they have space around them. They are not crowded. In addition, they do not need governments to keep order. That's why several anthropologists have called them 'anarchists'. They don't need governments or welfare provisions, although probably the rest of us do.

We have looked at nomadism before, but let's look more closely. On a scale of nomadism, we find that in fact it is *not* hunter-gatherers who tend to be nomadic, but in fact *farmers*. It may have been centuries ago, but the nomadic farmers of Europe did move from place to place. Also, cattle and sheep herders tend to migrate from place to place in search of better pastures, and in search of more land. In contrast, most hunter-gatherers remain pretty much where they were born. That is why humankind remains in southern and eastern Africa.

Africa is literally the natural home of *all* humanity. Of course, some humans did move to Australia. They moved on foot and on rafts or boats, but this took a great many thousands of years. Presumably, they never planned such a migration. It just happened! Those who arrived in Australia were simply the descendants of those who left Africa long before. The first Australian Aborigines could speak, but writing was unknown to them.

Hunter-gatherers recognize territories, but they give away the rights to use them. In a sense, they can be described as territorial, but this again is a matter of definition. Defining things and then debating about them is one of the foundations of social science. In the Kalahari, one anthropologist used to insist that the protection of a territory was 'natural'. Others disagreed. Definition often works like this: it is dependent on exact meaning. What is 'territorial' for one person may not be 'territorial' for everyone. Also, territoriality is a kind of relative concept.

Studies of hunter-gatherers show that they have considerable environmental knowledge. For example, both Ju/'hoan-si and Gwich'in (or Kutchin), know the names of hundreds of plants and animals. The Gwich'in live in the Yukon, in northern Canada, and they know about 400 species. They are famed for their beadwork, and they live mainly by hunting caribou. Let's think about that. How many species do you know?

Theories of hunter-gatherer society

There are many theories about the workings of hunter-gatherer society. One is called 'optimal foraging theory'. This theory predicts that organisms in general (including people) seek and consume the foods that contain the most calories, and that they spend the *least* amount of time they can in doing this. In other words, the idea coincides with the anthropologist Marshall Sahlins's vision of hunter-gatherers as 'the original affluent society'. In his book *Stone Age Economics*, first published is 1972, Sahlins wrote about how little effort is needed to hunt and gather. You just need lots of land, and a need *not* to accumulate property. What you have, you need to share or give away.

Hunter-gatherers display an extraordinary capacity for sharing. This is not necessarily just because they are good people, although they may be. It is because sharing is part of their cultural heritage. Sharing takes many forms. Within families people share, and often among hunter-gatherers the practice is extended across the band or across the ethnic group as a whole. In a sense, sharing is the opposite of accumulation. If hunter-gatherers share it is because it is culturally appropriate to do so. Typically, as in Sahlins's model, hunter-gatherers prefer to save time rather than wealth, and for this reason it is *time* that they accumulate. On the other hand, it is typical for Bushmen to carry a fairly empty tobacco pouch, and when someone asks for tobacco, it can be this fairly empty pouch (rather than one's full one) that is shown. I have seen this many times. People may know what is happening, but they don't let on.

In the Arctic the emphasis on seasonality has been prominent for a century. This is partly because of Marcel Mauss, a French anthropologist who wrote on seasonality among the Inuit. There was a *social* time of year (winter), and there was a time of *family*-based activities (summer). Such seasonal changes have ever since characterized descriptions of hunter-gatherer lifestyles. This is true not only in the Arctic, but right across the globe. Hunter-gatherers work *with* their environments to get the best from them. That is why hunter-gatherers still exist at all. A related is that of *the giving environment*. This was first proposed by Israeli anthropologist Nurit Bird-David. Basically, non-hunter-gatherers think in terms of *exploiting the environment*. Hunter-gatherers think instead in terms of the environment *giving* to them.

Bird-David was a student of James Woodburn, whose theory is a little different. Woodburn distinguishes two kinds of hunter-gatherers: those with an *immediate return* economy and those with a *delayed-return* one. In an immediate-return economy, people live off of what they can take. There is no investment in the future. They get their food, and they eat it on the spot. Or they give it to their fellow band members. Either way, it is eaten at most a day or two later. A delayed-return one does involve

Photo 6. Meat sharing among the Mbendjele

Photo by Jerome Lewis, Wikipedia entry 'hunter-gatherers', accessed 1 December 2019 planning ahead. For example, some hunter-gatherers plan ahead by building fishing traps, rather than just going fishing. Others build boats, which takes time. Most hunter-gatherers are immediate-return, but all non-hunter-gatherers have delayed-return economies. This puts the boundary between 'people like us' and 'other people' rather more towards the 'other people'. The extreme form of sharing that immediate-return hunter-gatherers have is rather rare.

These theories may be a little difficult to comprehend at first. Yet they do tell us a good deal, some of it familiar and some of it unfamiliar. Think about them and what they tell us about the ways hunters and gatherers are similar to us, and the ways in which they are different.

A personal note

A lot of people have asked me about the practicalities of fieldwork. The same questions emerge, so let me try to answer some of them.

Did I go hunting? Actually, I did try, but I was pretty useless! Food is shared, and I did share what I had, especially with the two boys pictured above. Did I eat the same food as they did? Pretty much, but what comes in tins is thought of as *gathered* rather than as *hunted*. For Bushmen gathered food only needs to be shared within the family, but hunted food has to be shared more widely. Did I travel with them? Yes, but I didn't have many possessions – just notebooks. I did have a vehicle though late in my fieldwork, and this proved useful in a couple of emergencies: for things like taking people to hospital.

Was it difficult? Actually, not at all. The most important thing for me was learning the Naro language. The language *is* extremely difficult and had never been written down before. But the Naro people were very helpful, and I did learn it fairly quickly. Yet when I left my own band, I was pretty much at sea: other Naro I met elsewhere didn't understand that I was actually *not* that proficient. Yet leaning at least a little of the language was the most important thing I did. It gave me at least a window into their way of thinking, as well as things to talk about!

6.

VIOLENCE AND PEACE

Sharing is one feature that typically identifies hunter-gatherers and distinguishes them from non-hunter-gatherers. Yet this is only one feature typical of this kind of society. Let's look at a few of these in more detail. Some you already have seen, others will perhaps need more explanation or thinking about.

- sharing, and a peaceful manner
- large territories for the size of the population
- great flexibility
- usually, a lack of social hierarchy (Northwest Coast societies are the exception)
- gender differences in ritual and in subsistence activities (usually, women gather and men hunt)
- a symbolic system based on binary oppositions, such as male/female

Beyond this, hunter-gatherers have a world order in which there are symbolic relations between levels, for example, gender difference is reflected in male and female attributes more broadly.

Many of these attributes are related. But just because they share, does that mean they are always peaceful?

The harmless people?

In her book *The Harmless People*, Elizabeth Marshall Thomas famously described Bushmen as peaceful and harmless. She emphasized their innocence and the lack of meaning harm to others, both within the community and toward outsiders. In contrast, in *The !Kung San*, Richard Lee calls attention to the high degree of conflict and verbal and physical abuse. The difference in the two accounts can't simply be because of regional difference or because of social change. Thomas's fieldwork was in the 1950s, and Lee's mainly in the 1960s and since. They did work in different parts of the Kalahari, but that's not the reason for the difference. Thomas was writing about the G/ui and Lee about the Ju/'hoan-si. Lee said that the murder rate among the Ju/'hoan-si is about the highest in the world.

Perhaps the difference was due in part to differences in perception. Perhaps Thomas was looking for a peaceful society, so she found one! She later did work with the Ju/'hoan-si, although her description comes from her work with the G/ui. The other major ethnographer of the Ju/'hoan-si was Thomas's mother, Lorna Marshall. She is the author of the famous paper about *sharing* among this people. Both groups live in relatively peaceful communities. And of course, they have no police forces. They are true anarchists: they live without government. Occasionally, they send troublemakers away though. They can do this because they have so much land, and the people who are forced to leave the community can go and live somewhere else. This would not work in a society like our own, but it does seem to work among both the Ju/'hoan-si and the G/ui.

So, maybe they share widely, but they also commit murder! Life can be complicated. The reasons for the differences here may result from what the anthropologists expected to find as much as what they did find. Conflict among the Ju/'hoan-si may simply be the result of living too close together in the dry season. Or maybe living too close to the anthropologists! Actually, I rather doubt that, but thinking about the nature of peace is important. It may not simply be a lack of conflict, but something deeper.

On a personal note, let me explain that my ancestor Thomas Barnard was a late seventeenth-century Quaker. He settled in a remote area of North America, and later he was murdered by Native Americans. I doubt if either he or his murderers were evil, or that his murder was justified.

Yet this story does tell us something about the idea of conflict. It can happen without intention.

Photo 7 shows a peaceful group in Malaysia. The photo was taken in 1905. But, we might ask, are they still a peaceful people?

Let's look at two groups now to try to consider this question: the Chewong and the Batek.

Photo 7. Peaceful people of Malaysia, 1905

Wikipedia entry, 'Orang Asli', accessed 1 December 2019

Two further examples: Chewong and Batek

Both the Chewong and the Batek live in Malaysia, and very near each other. Their way of life is very peaceful and much more like that described by Elizabeth Marshall Thomas than that described by Richard Lee.

The anthropologist who studied the Chewong is Signe Howell, who comes from Norway. She once told me that she had to explain to the Chewong that people in her country often live in flats or apartments. The Chewong were very rural and isolated, and they had never heard of this. They thought it was very funny, people all living in square boxes on top of each other! The Chewong, of course, live in a very different way from Norwegians. Their home is deep in the rainforest. They live in very small communities and are famous for their peaceful way of living. They say that social stratification, with a chief at the top, is part of the outside world and not part of their own. They believe that spirits live in everything: in plants, trees and flowers. They hunt, but they hunt in peace and never in anger. The title of her article in the book *Societies at Peace* says it all: 'To be angry is not to be human, but to be fearful is'. Outsiders, they say, are violent and are cheaters and thieves. Chewong do not behave in this way. It is not beyond coincidence that after she did fieldwork with the Chewong, Signe Howell chose a different Southeast Asian society for her next field project. She worked with the Lio of Indonesia. They are very different, not hunter-gatherers but cultivators, and not egalitarian but with a social hierarchy. This enabled her to compare the two peoples, and she found that she preferred living with the peaceful, egalitarian Chewong.

The Batek are another people of the Malaysian peninsula. Together the Chewong and the Batek are called the *orang asli*, which in the Malay language means the 'original people'. They were the hunter-gatherers of Malaysia long before other people came. The Batek have no notion that they *own* the land they live on. They just move around within their territories. In fact, few things are owned: only the combs that women keep or the blowpipes that men use in hunting. Like the Chewong, Batek are known for being very peaceful and for sharing everything they have, even the smallest pieces of food. The majority of people in Malaysia are Muslim, but when they tried to convert, one Batek said simply: 'We can't just forget our deities.'

So here we have societies at peace and each with a belief system that coincides with this way of living. The reason that the Chewong and the Batek can maintain this is that they believe that bad things come from the outside, and not from within their own communities. Maybe there is a lesson here for us all.

7.

LOOKING AFTER THE ENVIRONMENT

In 2019 Swedish teenager Greta Thunberg caught the word's attention. She started a strike at her school, to point out that the world faces a climate emergency. She met the Pope. She spoke at many venues, including at the House of Commons in the UK. She has even been nominated for the Nobel Peace Prize. What makes her different is that she recognized the climate emergency, and politicians didn't.

The people who best know their own environments are hunter-gatherers.

The environments that hunter-gatherers live in are very different, but each group will know their own environment very well. Richard Lee lists 220 species of plants known to the Ju/'hoan-si and of these 11 are as yet unknown to Western botany. As for animals, these people know about 58 species of mammals, and they also know dozens of other animals. Remember, they have always lived in sparsely populated parts of Africa, and relying on such a large number of plants and animals is not easy. No wonder it is said that they 'know their environment well'.

It is not only Bushmen. Other hunter-gatherers do too. The Gwich'in (formerly called the Kutchin), for example, know the names of over 400 different plants and animals! They live in the Canadian Yukon. Contrary to popular belief, hunter-gatherers haven't been pushed off the land of other groups: they live where they do because they need to survive on what they find. They know how to do that. Part of the reason for this is that they have lived where they do for millennia, and all this time they have subsisted by simple means. They may have only spears and bows and arrows, but these are enough for them to get what they need.

Communication?

The folklorist Megan Biesele notes that one key to understanding hunter-gatherers is to understand that communication is important. It is also shared: everyone has a say. She writes:

The most important achievement of hunting-gathering cultures through human history has been effective internal communication. These cultures have been able reliably, if on a small scale, to motivate and inform individuals as to what they must do to make group life continue. They have found successful ways to make decisions, coordinate activities, and suppress conflict. With low population levels they have remained in balance within their environments, which they change very little in order to live.

Perhaps smaller populations are the key. Or perhaps a way to coordinate activities, or simply to live without changing the environment. Whatever the exact solution, there is a hint here that hunters and gatherers know what they are doing while the rest of us don't.

We have seen this before. It is not police or governments that are necessary, but simply talking with one another. South Africa's national motto is in the language of the / Xam Bushmen: !Ke e: /xarra //ke. Officially it is translated 'Diverse people unite'. This is an allusion to some words in *The Communist Manifesto*, but the full meaning of their motto remains unknown to most South Africans. The / Xam language is now dead, but the words can actually mean something like: 'People who are different are talking to one another'. //Ke can mean either 'unite' or 'talk to one another'.

Protecting the environment

There is only one nation in the world that has protection of the environment enshrined in its Constitution. That nation is Namibia. Part of the reason is no doubt the time of Namibia's independence, 1990. Part of the reason too is the natural beauty of the country. But aren't all countries beautiful? Yes, of course. So why this one?

Photo 8. Desert environment, Namibia

In truth, hunter-gatherers are often not that good at protecting their environments. I have seen bits of paper and sweet wrappers dotted around the place in several parts of the Kalahari Desert. The Kalahari is a big place, bigger than France for example. The fact that it is so sparsely populated doesn't matter. Climate change is affecting everywhere in the world, and in particular global warming. Sea levels have gone up and down through the centuries. The problem now is that things are getting tough pretty much everywhere. One bit of paper or a sweet wrapper dropped here or there may not matter too much, especially in a place like that. Yet the effect is cumulative. Climate change is a very complex problem. They may not know it yet, but ultimately even hunter-gatherers living far inland are affected by it. The most valuable resource in the Kalahari is water: think about the seasonal cycle of the G/ui we saw in Figure 3. The Kalahari is becoming drier, and this will affect everything there.

Namibia was far ahead of other countries in protecting its resources. Let us hope that the rest of the world can catch up. Let us hope too that hunter-gatherers can take this on board. They may know their environments extremely well, but even they don't always look after them.

8.

ART, MUSIC AND RELIGION

A rt, music and religion are found almost everywhere, among hunter-gatherers as well as among other peoples. Let's explore some of the mystery of these three wonderful things.

Art

The earliest art we know about is the kind painted on the walls of caves. It may be older than we think, though. There is no way to tell, since our knowledge of the earliest art depends on what has survived. The earliest cave art in Africa was painted by around 25,000 years ago. Cave art is found just about on every continent, and everywhere it occurs it can be dated at least roughly. In addition to painting, rock art can include engraving: when images are carved into the rock. This is also very ancient, and certainly predates keeping livestock and cultivation.

Abstract art too may be very old. We know about etchings dated at around 100,000 years, and beadwork of a similar age. The earliest abstract art may be face painting.

Photo 9. Rock engraving

This has been dated variously to 270,000 or 170,000 years ago. Certainly, red ochre, which is probably what they used, can be dated to 160,000 years ago. In any case, hunter-gatherers today often love art, and some hunting and gathering peoples are very good at it. Both Bushmen and Australian Aborigines today produce art for the world market. Most of this is somewhat abstract, but it also makes use of symbols that are culturally significant to the artists and important in ritual.

The reason that art is found everywhere among hunter-gatherers tells us that it must be very old. In spite of simple

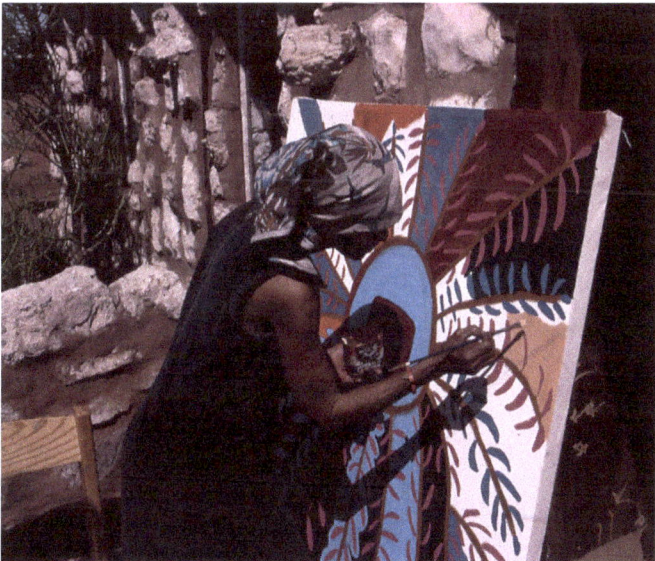

Photo 10. Painting today

technologies, hunter-gatherers seem always able to find time to draw, to paint, and to make things with wonderful beadwork. And with meaning.

Music

Music is similar. We have no way of knowing how old it is. Experts often speculate about such things, though. Some experts trace the beginning of language to the 'singing Neanderthals'. Maybe the earliest form of communication was *humming*. Even musical instruments are quite ancient. The 'Neanderthal flute' found in Slovenia dates from 42,000 years ago. Certainly people could sing before they could play the flute! In the Kalahari, traditional instruments include thumb piano, and other things, such as a one-stringed instrument where the string is tapped with a stick. There is also the *segaba*, a violin-like instrument that is borrowed from a neighbouring cultivating people. Where do they get the strings? From wire picked up from cultivating groups too.

Singing is very common among hunter-gatherers today, and it is often associated with rituals, like the 'medicine dance' among Kalahari Bushmen. The 'medicine' here is spiritual rather than physical. Men will work themselves up, often in their belief, with the help of a spirit of a dead person. Generally, the spirit will be unknown to them. In this ritual, women sing while man dance around them and go into a state of *trance*. Sometimes women will go into trance too, although this is much rarer. The singing

Photo 11. A musical bow

is unusual to us in the West. The music goes up and down in pitch. It is stylized and makes use of complex tunes and with different women singing different ones.

We find similar rituals among many hunting and gathering peoples, such as among Inuit and other Arctic groups where ritual trance performance is quite common and regarded as normal.

Religion

Probably most hunter-gatherers have a belief in a single god. Even before missionaries came, this seems to have been the case. In the early twentieth century, one Catholic priest from Germany, Father Wilhelm Schmidt, sent members of his order around the world to do studies of hunter-gatherers to prove that this was the case! In general, he was correct. However, there are exceptions. For example, the Australian Aborigines believe in a mythical 'Dreamtime', when the world was new and 'totems' symbolized each species and each clan. There is, then, no single religion among hunters and gatherers. And perhaps surprisingly to us, the flexibility that hunter-gatherers enjoy in their daily activities finds its way into religion too. They generally do not have differences in doctrine, but accept the ability of different people to believe whatever they like.

Apart from monotheism (a belief in one god), other common religions among hunter-gatherers are animism and shamanism. *Animism* is simply the idea that everything has 'spirit': rocks, trees and so on. We have just heard about totemism. *Totemism* is the belief in totems: spiritual entities that symbolize a clan, for example. The 'crocodile people' might believe that they are all related to an original crocodile. Totemism is common in Aboriginal Australia and the Subarctic, but otherwise is not general

Photo 12. An Inuit shaman (on the right), 1900

Wikipedia entry 'Inuit religion', accessed 1 December 2019

among hunter-gatherers. *Shamanism* is found in many places, especially in Asia, South America and the Arctic. This religion regards some people, *shamans*, in a special position, as ritual specialists with unusual powers. They can become bears or foxes, for example, and travel across the sky. Such travel is found in the belief systems of many hunter-gatherer groups.

A number of anthropologists, though, don't like the idea of classifying all shamans or totems as being alike. There are many different such things, and quite a lot of variation among the religions that recognize them. Shamans can be either male or female, and some training is needed before a person becomes one. In other words, it is a special profession. The word 'shaman' comes from a religion found in Siberia, and the word 'totem' is from Ojibwa, a language found in southern Canada near the Great Lakes.

The diversity in all these things hints at the great time depth that separates the world's hunter-gatherer peoples. Perhaps their flexibility in social organization also hints at the tolerance they have of different points of view: even in religious belief.

The story of the moon and the hare

Many stories have a symbolic dimension. We usually call them 'myths'. Let me relate one now. This one is the Bushman version, but similar stories or myths are found among other hunter-gatherers too. This version is really all about the origin of death, as well as the hare's split lip.

> The moon sent the hare to tell the people that those who are ill will be fine. But the hare got it wrong! He said that when people die, they will live again, just as the moon does each month.
>
> And so the moon was angry! He said: 'Don't go getting things wrong again.' The moon then hit the hare on the mouth and told him not to speak, and to go and live as a wild animal. The hare could not live among people any more. He had to sleep in the bush, and when he died he would stay dead.

That's a very brief version, but the idea is pretty clear. Many written versions have the word 'moon' beginning with a capital letter. He is almost a god-like figure, and he is reborn each month as the old moon fades and the new moon comes up in his place. Note the gender! Among Bushmen, the moon is usually masculine and the sun is feminine, the opposite as we find in the West. But it does depend on the specific Bushman language. My own skills as a Naro-speaker have never been very good, so I didn't collect much folklore. Also, since everyone had already heard the stories, the narrator usually left stuff out! How can one record a story unless it is complete?

Can you find any other symbols in this story or myth? Indeed is there a difference between a story and a myth? In many Bushman languages the same word is used for both.

9.

UNIVERSAL KINSHIP

I was once able to spend a short time in Australia. There I met a group of Australian Aborigines, or Native Australians. I knew about 'universal kinship' because I had encountered it in Botswana. This means that everyone classifies every other person as 'kin'. There are no 'non-kin'. Everyone *in the whole of society* classifies everyone else. If you have the same name as my sister, then I call you 'sister' and I cannot marry you!

At first, the Aborigines I met thought I must have been *initiated* as an Aborigine because I knew this principle. In fact, it was just the theory of such things that I knew. Both Aboriginal societies and most Bushman societies have such a principle. It seems strange to us, but it is commonplace in these, and many other, hunter-gatherer societies. For a hunter-gatherer, in general everyone is kin. This affects every member of their society, and even some outsiders. Even I (and every other anthropologist) is caught up in this when we are given a name and therefore a local identity as a member of their community.

In my own case, the Bushman name is what is important. This may not be true in all Bushman societies, but it is true in the case of the Naro (among whom I lived for about two years) and the neighbouring Ju/'hoan-si. The Naro live in central Botswana. My Naro name is !A/e. I think I was named after another !A/e, who was absent during my first year in Naro country. He could also speak English, since he was half Naro and half English. Normally, a Naro bears the name of a grandparent or an uncle or aunt. Names cycle down the generations, and if I meet another !A/e he is my 'grandfather'. Not only that, but his sister is my 'sister', and I have to treat her as if she were my own sister, and so on! Every anthropologist who has worked with northern

Photo 13. Bushman child being introduced to his 'grandfather'

Bushmen has experienced this, although in southern areas it is different.

Let me then explain 'universal kinship'. This means the *necessity* to classify everyone you meet as 'kin'. You have to treat them as kin, and in fact as members of particular kinship categories. This is normal among Australian Aborigines, Inuit, Bushmen and among many other hunter-gatherer peoples. It is *not* normal, of course, in most other societies, including Western ones.

Australian Aboriginal kinship

Australian Aboriginal kinship is 'universal', and Aborigines have the most complicated kinship systems on earth. As famous French anthropologist Claude Lévi-Strauss once said,

> ... we know that mankind is about one or two million years old, but while we are ready to grant man this great antiquity, we are not ready to grant man a continuous thinking capacity during this enormous length of time. I see no reason why mankind should have waited until recent times to produce minds of the caliber of a Plato or an Einstein. Already, over

two or three hundred thousand years ago, there were probably men of a similar capacity, who were probably not applying their intelligence to the solution of the same problems as these more recent thinkers; instead, they were probably more interested in kinship!

Of course today we would say 'humankind' and 'humanity' (rather than 'man'), but otherwise the words of Lévi-Strauss hold true.

Let me throw you in at the deep end. Have a look at the Kariera system, which is found in Western Australia.

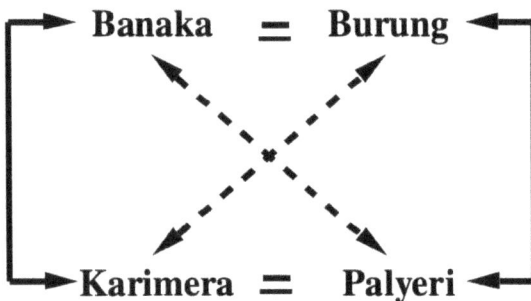

Figure 5. The four Kariera sections

In Figure 5, the equals sign means 'to marry', and the arrows connect a mother to her children. The dotted lines across the middle connect fathers to their children. The way to read the figure is as follows. 'Male Banaka marries female Burung; the children are Palyeri. Male Palyeri marries female Karimera; the children are Banaka.' Illustrated here is a 'four section system', but even more complicated is an 'eight section system'. The classic four-section system is called Kariera, after the tribe near Australia's west coast that have such a system. The classic eight-section one is called Aranda, after a people who live in the interior of the continent. Then there is Murngin, named after a people who live in north-central Australia. Today they are called Yolngu, but in any case Yolngu (or Murngin) is the most complicated of all, with, in their understanding, something like 32 sections!

The systems have all evolved over time, and groups far away from each other can sometimes fit their systems together, for example when a person wants to marry someone from far away. Experts suggest that the systems evolved to their present form only a few centuries ago. But do people really choose their spouses in this way? Not really, because they can opt to change the category instead! That way, the constraints are not as great as one might think. In theory then, everyone marries 'correctly'.

Languages can be grouped into *language families*. These 'families' are in constant but quite slow change. For this reason you may have a slightly different pronunciation (or even use quite different words) from ones used by your grandmother. Language families only survive for about 7,000 or 8,000 years. Before that, it is pretty much impossible to reconstruct what people might have been saying. Think French and Spanish for example, or German and English. All these languages are in fact related, but still several hundred or even a few thousand years apart. Australia was first settled around 60,000 years ago. Think how many languages have been spoken there. How many still are? Not as many as you might think.

Australia was once home to the *first sailors*. Their sailing may at first have been accidental though. Aborigines came to Australia after their ancestors made it, over several thousand years, from Africa, across Asia, to Australia. The distance from Southeast Asia across the Timor Sea to mainland Australia was, in the past, nearly 100 kilometres. Travel from Africa was, of course, on foot. But not to Australia; the first Australians must have used rafts or boats. Possibly even a single boat or raft. That trip may never have been planned, but surely it was made.

In their many millennia in Australia, Aborigines devised the complicated kinship systems the world has ever seen. It is difficult to call them 'complex' here because Lévi-Strauss used the word 'complex' for systems like our own, which have an infinite number of possible spouses. In Australia, marriage is constrained by complicated rules governing such choices. But it is not quite that complicated: just four choices in the Kariera case, and to marry the wrong one would be to commit incest! Strange as it may seem, kinship systems seem to become more regular through time, and the Kariera system is a good example of this. We do not know what the system looked like in the past, but it is now complete and completely well formed.

Beyond Australia

So, as Lévi-Strauss implied, this is what hunter-gatherers do when not hunting and gathering! They devise and practise using very complicated kinship systems. Admittedly, the kinship systems of Pygmies, Bushmen, Inuit and many other hunter-gatherer peoples are much simpler. Yet the principles are similar. Hunter-gatherers may have simple technology, but they are anything but simple in the way they relate to one another. The examples I have given here —the Kalahari and Australia—are just those of my travels.

Hunter-gatherers also live in other places too: the Ona and Yahgan of the southern tip of South America, various peoples of Siberia and so on.

They do not all have universal kinship, but one thing all these places have in common is that they are isolated from the outside world.

10.

THREE CASE STUDIES:
BUSHMEN, ABORIGINES, INUIT

I have chosen three case studies to illustrate the hunter-gatherer way of life: Bushmen, Aborigines and Inuit. I have a little experience of all three, although the Bushmen are by far the people I know best because I have spent many years with them. Let's start then with them.

Bushmen

The Bushmen or San live in southern Africa. As I have mentioned, the label for the group is in dispute. I usually refer to them as Bushmen, but they are also known as San, Kua, Basarwa and by other names. The word San is common in South Africa. The word Basarwa can be troublesome; the usual form used to be Masarwa. Then a schoolchild alerted us to the fact that these are indeed *people*, and the word was changed. In the Tswana language, *Ba-* is the plural prefix for humans (as on the doors of rest rooms, *basadi*, ladies; *banna*, gents). Using *Ma-* instead would imply that they are more like trees!

Sometimes I do use other labels; it depends on my audience. Some Ju/'hoan-si call *all* Bushmen Ju/'hoan-si. Similarly with Kua. Some use that word to mean *all* *Bushmen*. Others use it to mean just one tiny group. Why should there be such disagreement among the people themselves? Of course, each group knows who they are, and there is no agreed word for *Bushman* in any Bushman language. The use of any of these words can imply that they are a people of low status. Frankly, that is how many think of Bushmen.

However, as we have seen Bushmen are as sophisticated as anyone else. Their knowledge of plants and animals is incomparable. Their ability to cope with harsh climatic conditions is legendary, and they do this with the simplest of technology. Bushmen speak many different languages, and some can speak several of them.

And as we have seen, some of these are very difficult ones, and rather more difficult to learn than English.

We have seen examples of their settlement patterns. They use these effectively to make the most of their harsh environments. They know where to find food, and they do this not only with little effort. They work for their living, but they do this with skill and efficiency. Even in times of drought, they can cope. It is people who grow crops and keep livestock who have problems with drought, not the hunters and gatherers.

Aborigines

The Aborigines are, in many ways, similar. There are differences though. In religion, for example, Bushmen believe in one god. They cure each other through trance dances in which spirits are invoked to assist them.

Aborigines, on the other hand, believe in a mythical Dreamtime. Their spirits are *totems* that represent the species of each clan. They trace descent particularly through males, but some groups trace through females instead. Sometimes whole societies are divided into two groups, into what are known by anthropologists as *moieties*. This word is from the French for 'half', and the division is important in tracing kinship. A person must marry into the *other* half, never taking his or her spouse from their own half.

Aborigines do not use bows and arrows, but only have spears. Some groups are said to be quite violent, and spear throwing is not unknown. Above all, Aborigines defend their territories, which are exclusive to the group that owns them. What is unknown though is how far back in the past these customs can be traced. Were they always there, or only after Captain James Cook landed in 1770? We do not know. If they are violent today, their violence was probably no worse than that of the First World War, or for that matter, the Second World War.

The Aborigines were the first people to live in Australia. The same word is used for many other *first peoples*, but when it refers to the first people of Australia it is always capitalized. *Aborigines* in general are simply the first people of wherever they settled. But in Canada they are known as First Nations. Why such a fuss? It's because these things are important to people who are downtrodden or underprivileged. That's one reason why in Australia the word Aborigines is always spelled with a capital 'A'.

The Aborigines arrived in Australia perhaps 60,000

Photo 14. Nineteenth-century engraving of an Aboriginal camp, 1876

Wikipedia entry 'hunter-gatherers', accessed 1 December 2019

year ago. The white Australians only arrived much later, with Captain Cook. Later settlers have been arriving ever since then. So, you may ask, what did the first Australians do? Well, they had to learn to hunt and gather in very difficult surroundings. They learned to use the tools they had, and they developed new ones, like the boomerang. They got to Australia in the first place across a land bridge that connected Southeast Asia to the Australian continent. That land bridge has long since been under water, although it is known that part of the original journey will have involved a short sea voyage by boat or raft. The sea around Australia has a deep channel that must have been crossed at some point in the distant past. The earliest Australians may have been only a tiny group, but through the 60,000 years the population expanded enormously.

Estimates vary, but experts estimate that the total population of Australia when Europeans arrived was about 300,000. That's about one person for every 25 square kilometres, or every 10 square miles. Some parts of Australia were more populous than others, of course. The area near modern Sydney had a greater population than the interior, and desert areas had much smaller populations than along the coast. It all depended on the *carrying capacity* of the land: how many people could find enough food to live there.

Aborigines speak many different languages and have very different cultures. Yet among the things they do have in common is the belief in the Dreamtime. It is said that this concept is very difficult for others to understand. It refers to a time when the world was created and when each people gained knowledge of the land and its sacred places. This is central to Aboriginal religion, which in spite of social and political changes over the last 250 years is still present. What is sacred to them takes a long time to disappear. Is it not their right to believe what they wish?

Aborigines perform elaborate funerals. These involve

Photo 15. Aborigines fishing for crabs

not just burial, but sometimes *reburial*. They dig up the body about ten years after death and bury it again. On the other hand, we know from archaeological evidence that cremation was known and performed in the distant past. We know a lot about Aborigines but there is still much we don't know, especially about the long history of their time in Australia.

Inuit

My wife is fond of the Arctic. I had been to northern Norway a few times, and eventually we had the chance to travel on board a ship bound for eastern Greenland. We were only there as tourists, and only briefly. But really, this mattered little. The thrill of this experience was enlightening. I got to see first hand things I had only known from my anthropological reading.

Our landing site is called *Ittoqqortoormiit*, and the population is only 450. Most are professional seal hunters. Still, it is the largest village in eastern Greenland; the total population of that half of the island is only around 600. The vast majority of the people of Greenland (still fewer than 60,000) live on the western side. If the language of the Naro Bushmen is troublesome, that of Inuit is even more difficult: one dialect of it is supposed to have more than 450 different parts of speech! The language is called Inuktitut (person–speech). Again, there is more complexity in the language than there is in the technology, if I can put it that way. We in the West have computers and so on; Greenlanders seem to have complex grammar instead!

The Inuit are the people once called Eskimo. Why the name change? Probably you can guess. Most Inuit do prefer to be called 'Inuit'. The word 'Eskimo' is also very common, and it may be preferred in some areas, especially in Alaska where the word *Inuit* is unknown. However, *Inuit* and *Eskimo* both seem to be actually foreign words. Its exact meaning is not known, even in Canada or Greenland. It is much the same as with San and Bushmen. Neither of these words is found in the places where San or Bushmen live. Think about this: it is an interesting problem. The people of the Aleutian Islands, which lie off the southern tip of Alaska, are called Yupik: the same word as in Siberia. What we *call* people is a difficult issue. Partly, this is a problem of political correctness. But getting the right term is often difficult, especially when opinions differ. Generally though, we are safe with 'hunter-gatherers'.

Like the Aborigines, the people of North America got there by travelling across a land bridge. It once connected Siberia to the North American continent, tens of thousands of years ago. Estimates vary, but current research suggests that the very first American inhabitants arrived in North America about 50,000 BP. They then moved south all the way to South America. The original peoples of the Americas later developed agriculture, but those of the far north, who came more recently, remained hunters and gatherers. The Inuit are descended from those more recent peoples, and their arrival in the Americas can be dated to perhaps 6,000 years ago. We know this because of studies done by geologists of sea level changes. The changes in sea level were caused by melting and freezing of the ice in the

Photo 16. Eastern Greenland

Bering Sea. The earliest Eskimo or Inuit may have lived in grasslands, but eventually the grasslands turned colder.

So, Inuit is the term for the hunter-gatherers of northern Canada and Greenland. These are very remote places, and few people have ever been there. Northern Canada and Greenland are, of course, very cold. The people who live there are among the last hunter-gatherers to settle. Today, they live in the most inhospitable place on earth.

On the other hand, Bushmen and Aborigines have been in their present locations for a very long time. All these peoples are well adapted, and Inuit traditionally dress for the cold. They wear parkas or anoraks, for example: these are a kind of coat that keeps out the rain, wind and cold. The very word *parka* is from the Aleutian Islands. The word *anorak* is from the Greenlandic language. Another Greenlandic word you probably know is *kayak*. This is a kind of small boat, with just enough space for one individual. It too is adapted for use in the cold.

Probably most everyone knows that Inuit have a great many words for snow. Or do they really have that many? Actually, they have an uncountable number! This is because the definition of a 'word' depends on people recognizing it as such. Also, the grammar of the language prevents any easy understanding or translation. For example, in Inuktitut, specifically the dialect of the people of Nunavut in Canada, *tusaatsiarunnanngittualuujunga* means 'I cannot hear very well.' This long word is composed of the root *tusaa*, 'to hear', plus five suffixes meaning 'well – be able to – not – very much'. The last suffix means 'first person singular present indicative non-specific'. Inuit languages are *polysynthetic*. This means that bits of a word have no meaning in isolation. It's a bit like looking for the meaning of the *–s* in the English word 'cats'. Yes, *–s* is what makes the word plural, but without the rest of the word it has no meaning.

Photo 17. 'Community of igloos', 1865

From Charles Francis Hall's *Arctic Researches and Life among the Esquimaux*, 1865. Wikipedia entry 'igloo', accessed 1 December 2019

The traditional religion was shamanism. This is the idea that people can communicate with spirits or use spirits to help them. Inuit believe that they can *become* bears or wolves. Naming is important, so much so that a child without a name is not yet thought of as human. For this reason, a new-born child was sometimes left out on the ice to die. This was not thought of as murder, for the child was not yet thought of as a human being. However, feuding is not unknown, and killing people for various reasons is found among Inuit, as among other peoples. The person who dies, it is believed, can return later as a new person and slotted into the kinship system much as before. The soul, they say, can be recycled. They believe this about animals too, and for this reason they sometimes say that a hunter kills because an animal *wants to* be killed.

For an interesting take on the Inuit way of life, see Jean Briggs's book *Never in Anger*. Briggs, an anthropologist, was doing research in Uktuhikhalingmiut in northern Nunavut. She once lost her temper with the family that had taken her in, so she was left alone for months! No-one wanted to speak to her, because to express anger in Uktuhikhalingmiut is taboo. Perhaps we should never to too quick to judge people by our own standards.

Conclusion

In these three examples, we see the essence of what it means to be a hunter and gatherer. On the downside, we also see the problems hunter-gatherers face. They live in a world that today is dominated by non-hunter-gatherers. Many former hunters and gatherers have taken up other pursuits. They no longer hunt and gather for all their food. They fish; they herd animals; they grow crops. This mixed way of life has become normal.

Yet the hunting way of life is the original human way. *All* human societies began as hunter-gatherer societies. Can the world's remaining hunter-gatherers then retain their ideas of sharing, or their peaceful nature? Or even their ability to live in peace, with the ability to share what they have? If these things are beneficial *for all*, then why are *we* so stingy? Why can't the rest of us live as they do? That is for you to think about.

TOPICS FOR DISCUSSION

1. Bushmen give things very freely, but they have very few possessions. How easy is it to *give* like a Bushman? Could you do that?

2. Do you share what you have? How widely do you share, and what kind of things? Could you get away without sharing?

3. By definition, hunter-gatherers kill for a living. Most of us do not, but we eat animals killed by others. Could you kill for a living?

4. Nearly all hunter-gatherers live in remote parts of the world. Bushmen, Aborigines and Inuit are important examples. If you were to take up this lifestyle, on which continent you choose to live? Why?

5. Hunters and gatherers live without government and without the police. Is this a good thing? Are you able to live without these things?

6. Hunter-gatherers also live with simple technology: spears, bows and arrows, and so on. We live with computers and mobile phones. Could you give these up?

7. In Western society these days, it is unfashionable to throw away plastic. Too much of it ends up in the oceans, whether as great big chunks of a micro-beads that fish will eat. This means that when we eat fish, we are probably eating micro-beads of plastic! Clearly, this is not sustainable for the environment. What do you throw away?

    This is a very big question: what can we do about it? Might it also be affecting the few hunter-gatherers that remain in the world? Would it be better if more people were able to return to a hunter-gatherer lifestyle? Indeed can we actually do this? If hunter-gatherers need so much land, is there enough of it to allow a return to that way of life? Even if fishing is allowed, won't contamination of the world's water resources be a problem?

8. Try drawing up a table to show the differences between living in an urban, industrialized society and living in a hunter-gatherer society.

9. All hunting and gathering societies are confronted with change. Perhaps all peoples are. But is change always inevitable? What do you think is truly important for these people? What has to be discarded, and what can they retain? What about values? Which is more important, accumulating wealth or having more free time? And ultimately, what can we learn from *them*?

SOURCES AND SUGGESTIONS FOR FURTHER READING

1. Introduction: We are all hunters and gatherers?

It is not usual in this series to have full details of difficult scientific literature. However, in case if you are interested the recent paper that brought to light humanity's origins is: Jean-Jacque Hublin *et al.* 2017. 'New fossils from Jebel Irhoud, Morocco and the pan-African origin of *Homo sapiens*', *Nature* 546: 289–292.

Table 1 is based on material I have presented before, in *Social Anthropology and Human Origins* (2011), *Genesis of Symbolic Thought* (2012) and *Language in Prehistory* (2016). All were published in Cambridge, and around the world, by Cambridge University Press. The quotation I referred to is from the 'Preface' to *Man the Hunter*. Richard B. Lee and Irven DeVore (eds.), 1968, *Man the Hunter*, Chicago: Aldine, page ix.

2. The label 'hunters and gatherers'

The best work on human origins is Chris Stringer, 2011, *The Origin of Our Species*, London: Allen Lane.

Figure 2 is schematic, but it is based on material in several sources. Among them is Richard B. Lee, 2013, *The Dobe Ju/'hoansi* (fourth, International edition), London: Wadsworth, Cengage Learning. Figure 3, also schematic, is based on George B. Silberbauer's work, 1981, *Hunter and Habitat in the Central Kalahari Desert*, Cambridge: Cambridge University Press.

3. Could you live as a hunter-gatherer?

Table 2 and Table 3 are based on material first presented in Alan Barnard, 2007, 'From Mesolithic to Neolithic modes of thought', *Proceedings of the British Academy* 144: 5-19.

The quotation from Lee and DeVore is from the dust-jacket of their (1976) *Kalahari Hunter-Gatherers: Studies of the !Kung San and Their Neighbors*, Cambridge, MA: Harvard University Press. The reference to Thomas Hobbes is to *Leviathan*, edited by Richard Tuck, Cambridge: Cambridge University Press (1991). It was first published in 1651. The reference to Adam Smith is to his *Lectures on Jurisprudence*, edited by R.L. Meek, D.D. Raphael and P.G. Stein. Indianapolis: Liberty Fund (1982). It was written in 1762-63.

4. Band societies

The idea of 'band societies' was first promoted by Julian H. Steward in the 1930s and 1950s. His classic text was published in 1955 and was called *Theory of Culture Change: The Methodology of Multilinear Evolution*, Urbana, IL: University of Illinois Press. Elman R. Service's key works were published in 1962 and 1966. These were *Primitive Social Organization: An Evolutionary Perspective*, New York: Random House, 1962. *The Hunters*, Englewood Cliffs, NJ: Prentice-Hall, 1966.

5. Sharing and giving

Figure 4 is loosely based on a diagram that appears in my book, *Bushmen: Kalahari Hunter-Gatherers and Their Descendants*, Cambridge: Cambridge University Press, (2019), p. 74.

There are many texts on this theme. Among the best are Lorna Marshall, 1961, 'Sharing, talking, and giving: relief of social tensions among !Kung Bushmen'. *Africa* 31: 231-49. This article has been reprinted several times. Polly Wiessner, 1982, 'Risk, reciprocity, and social influence on !Kung San economics', in Eleanor Leacock and Richard Lee (eds.), *Politics and history in band societies*, Cambridge: Cambridge University Press, pp. 61-84. Thomas Widlok,

2017, *Anthropology and the economy of sharing*, London: Routledge. These three sources all deal with Bushman economics. This should not be surprising, since Bushmen are perhaps the best known people when it comes to sharing and giving. Finally, see Marshall Sahlins, 1974, *Stone Age Economics*, especially Chapter 1, 'The original affluent society', pp. 1-39.

6. Violence and peace

Again, the sources are numerous. One I recommend is Kirk M. Endicott and Karen L. Endicott. 2008, *The Headman Was a Woman: The Gender Egalitarian Batek of Malaysia*, Long Grove, IL: Waveland Press. The Endicotts are a husband and wife team who have done research in Malaysia. Kirk Endicott also wrote the chapter in Lee and Daly's *The Cambridge Encyclopedia of Hunters and Gatherers*, 'The Batek of peninsular Malaysia', pp. 298-302. The quotation is from that, page 301.

Another who has worked in Malaysia is Signe Howell. See, for example, her edited volume, Signe Howell and Roy Willis (eds.), 1989, *Societies at Peace: Anthropological Perspectives*, London: Routledge. She wrote the chapter 'To be angry is not to be human, but to be fearful is: Chewong concepts of human nature', pp. 45-59.

7. Looking after the environment

The quotation from Megan Biesele is from her 1986 article 'How hunter-gatherers' stories "make sense": semantics and adaptation', *Cultural Anthropology* 1(2): 157-70, page 157. On South Africa's motto, see Alan Barnard, 2003, '!Ke e: /xarra //ke—Multiple origins and multiple meanings of the motto.' *African Studies* 62: 243-50.

The material from Richard Lee is from Richard Borshay Lee, 1979, *The !Kung San: Men, Women, and Work in a Foraging Society*, Cambridge: Cambridge University Press, pp. 464-73.

8. Art, music and religion

A great deal has been written on cave art. For example, J.D. Lewis-Williams, 1981, *Believing and Seeing: Symbolic Meanings in Southern San rock Paintings*, London: Academic Press. Lewis-Williams has also written a number of other books on the subject, but this one is my favourite.

Music is the subject of much work too. For example, Iain Morley's chapter, 'Implications of music in hunter-gatherer societies', contained within Iain Morley, 2013, *The Prehistory of Music: Human Evolution, Archaeology, and the Origins of Musicality*, Oxford: Oxford University Press.

As for religion, one paper I like is Mathias Guenther, 1979, 'Bushman religion and the (non)sense of anthropological theory of religion', *Sociologus* 29(2): 102-32. Otherwise, remember that many hunter-gatherers believe in a single God. Others have shamanic beliefs and place one individual, who is believed to have special powers, above the others. See, for example, Margaret Stutley, 2003, *Shamanism: An Introduction*, London: Routledge.

9. Universal kinship

I invented the term 'universal kinship' back in the 1970s. Possibly it was not the best phrase, but it stuck. In fact most hunter-gatherers have it, and most non-hunter-gatherers don't have it. See Alan Barnard, 1978, 'Universal systems of kin categorization', *African Studies* 37: 69-81.

The quotation from Claude Lévi-Strauss is from his 1969 work *The Elementary Structures of Kinship* (second edition), London: Eyre and Spottiswoode, page 351. The French original dates from 1949.

The best examples of universal kinship are among Australian Aborigines. See Kenneth Maddock, 1973, *The Australian Aborigines: A Portrait of Their Society*, London: Allen Lane The Penguin Press.

10. Three case studies: Bushmen, Aborigines, Inuit

On Bushmen, see my own *Bushmen: Kalahari Hunter-Gatherers and Their Descendants*, Cambridge: Cambridge University Press (2019).

On Aborigines, there is Kenneth Maddock, 1973, *The Australian Aborigines: A Portrait of Their Society*, London: Allen Lane The Penguin Press. This is a bit complicated, but then so is Aboriginal kinship! There are also many classic books dating from the nineteenth and early twentieth centuries.

On Inuit or Eskimo, see Ernest S. Burch, Jr. 1988, *The Eskimos,* Norman, OK: University of Oklahoma Press. Burch uses the term 'Eskimos' because his fieldwork is in Alaska, where the term 'Inuit' is unknown. The note on language is from the Wikipedia entry 'Inuit languages'. Another interesting book is *Never in Anger: Portrait of an Eskimo Family*, by Jean L. Briggs, 1970, Cambridge MA: Harvard University Press.

BOOKS

There are a number of good books about hunter-gatherers. Some of my own favourites are listed below. But if you want to learn more about anthropology in general, I can recommend this one:

Ingold, Tim (2018) *Anthropology: Why It Matters*, Cambridge: Polity Press.
His is written mainly for young people who are thinking of taking up the subject at university.

Other relevant books include:

Barnard, Alan (2016) *Language in Prehistory*, Cambridge: Cambridge University Press.
This is about language, but it also contains a good deal of information on its beginnings among hunters and gatherers. They were the people who invented language!

Barnard, Alan (ed.) (2004) *Hunter-Gatherers in History, Archaeology and Anthropology*, Oxford: Berg Publishers.
A collection of writings by British, Japanese and Russian writers, showing differences in approach. A bit technical in parts, but appeal to some readers. Ironically, it is Japanese anthropologists who are at the forefront of hunter-gatherer studies.

Bettinger, Robert L., Raven Garvey and Shannon Tushingham (2015) *Hunter-Gatherers: Archaeological and Evolutionary Theory* (Second Edition), New York: Springer.
Mainly on archaeology, but very interesting.

Bicchieri, M.G. (ed.) (1988) *Hunters and Gatherers Today: A Socioeconomic Study of Eleven Such Cultures in the Twentieth Century*, Prospect Heights, IL: Waveland Press.
This is actually a reprint. The original was published in 1972, and the book covers Inuit, Canadian First Nations peoples, Aborigines and Bushmen as well as others. My favourite among the texts.

Brody, Hugh (2001) *The Other Side of Eden: Hunter-Gatherers, Farmers and the Shaping of the World*, London: Faber and Faber.
Mainly about Inuit, but also comparative and with reflections on the West. This is an easier read than many other relevant books.

Burch, Ernest S., Jr. and Linda J. Ellanna (eds.) (1994) *Key Issues in Hunter-Gatherer Research*, Oxford: Berg Publishers.
A famous collection with an emphasis on social development. It comes from a conference held Fairbanks, Alaska in 1990.

Cummings, Vicki (2013) *The Anthropology of Hunter-Gatherers: Key Themes for Archaeologists*, London: Bloomsbury.
Nice and clear, mainly archaeology.

Cummings, Vicki, Peter Jordan and Marek Zvelebil (eds.) (2014) *The Oxford Handbook of the Archaeology and Hunter-Gatherers*, Oxford: Oxford University Press.
This is a very large book. Again, mainly for people interested in archaeology.

Endicott, Kirk M. and Karen L. Endicott (2008) *The Headman Was a Woman: The Gender Egalitarian Batek of Malaysia*, Long Grove, IL: Waveland Press.
A nice book on these gender-egalitarian people, covering the period from 1975 to more recent times. Provocative, as well as informative, for those interested in gender equality.

Kelly, Robert L (2013) *The Lifeways of Hunter-Gatherers: The Foraging Spectrum*, Cambridge: Cambridge University Press.
The second edition of a 1995 classic. Emphasizes hunter-gatherer diversity. Hunter-gatherers are in fact very diverse, as they occupy some of the most difficult (and different) environments on earth.

Kusimba, Sibel Barut (2003) *African Foragers: Environment, Technology, Interactions*, Walnut

Creek, CA: AltaMira Press.
An excellent African view, mainly archaeology but with good discussion too of symbolism and exchange. These are important themes in hunter-gatherer studies.

Lee, Richard Borshay (1979) *The !Kung San: Men, Women, and Work in a Foraging Society*, Cambridge: Cambridge University Press.
A very big and detailed book, but well worth thumbing through!

Lee, Richard B. (2013) *The Dobe Ju/'hoansi* (fourth, International edition), London: Wadsworth, Cengage Learning.
An excellent overview of this African people: the Ju/'hoan-si are the people formerly known as the !Kung. Why the name change? Partly it is due to the choice of the Ju/'hoan-si themselves: the name means 'the real people'. The book covers the work of many different ethnographers.

Lee, Richard B. and Richard Daly (eds.) (1999) *The Cambridge Encyclopedia of Hunters and Gatherers*, Cambridge: Cambridge University Press.
More than 500 pages of text. Even if now a little dated, it covers most everything you might want to know about the traditional ways of hunter-gatherers.

Lee, Richard B. and Irven DeVore (eds.) (1968) *Man the Hunter*, Chicago: Aldine.

A great classic in anthropology, based on a 1966 conference: the one at which Marshall Sahlins first questioned the 'advances' of non-hunter-gatherer peoples. This book in general helped to debunk the theory that hunter-gatherers have to spend all day, every day, in subsistence pursuits.

Maddock, Kenneth (1973) *The Australian Aborigines: A Portrait of Their Society*, London: Allen Lane.

An excellent book on Aboriginal traditions. Quite technical in parts, especially on kinship, but then Australian Aborigines have the most complicated kinship systems on earth!

Panter-Brick, Catherine, Robert H. Layon and Peter Rowley-Conwy (eds.) (2001) *Hunter-Gatherers: An Interdisciplinary Perspective*, Cambridge: Cambridge University Press.

Covers many facets of hunter-gatherer life: ecology, archaeology, language, biology and other things.

Tanaka, Jiro (2014) *The Bushmen: A Half-Century Chronicle of Transformations in Hunter-Gatherer Life and Ecology*, Tokyo: Kyoto University Press / Melbourne: Trans Pacific Press.

Tanaka and his team spent nearly 50 years in the

Central Kalahari, and here they tell the tale of social change and forced migration.

Thomas, Elizabeth Marshall (1959) *The Harmless People*, London: Secker and Warburg
The classic vision of Bushmen as a peaceful set of peoples. Thomas describes mainly the G/ui here.

ALTERNATIVE BOOKS

Almost every book in the list above concerns hunter-gatherers. But for an alternative view, try these two, as well as other works by these writers. Marshall Sahlins is an eminent anthropologist. During a sabbatical in Paris in 1968 he turned economic anthropology on its head: he wrote a famous essay called 'The original affluent society', which is contained within his book *Stone Age Economics*. In it he shows the fallacy of the view that abandoning the hunter-gatherer lifestyle necessarily lead to advances for humankind. It did not! Hunter-gatherers actually spend less time, not more, in subsistence-related activities than do cultivators. Not only that, but their lifestyle is such that they fare better in times of drought and food shortage. Ever wonder why hunter-gatherers tend to occupy deserts and jungles?

Along the same lines, years later, George C. Scott argues against the view that domestication advanced civilization. Yes it did, but it also lead to forced labour and ultimately to slavery. His view is essentially an anarchist one. Again, he forces us to rethink what we have long been taught. He has written several books in this mould, but the key one is *Against the Grain*. Watch out though: the same title has been used by other writers!

Which would you prefer: a life of forced labour or one of easy living, with a guarantee of free time? The advantages of agriculture are vastly outweighed by the disadvantages. Yes, agriculture brings more wealth, at least for some, but at what cost? If you ever wonder why hunter-gatherers occupy deserts, it is because they need much more land than cultivators. This must spark a debate among your classmates! Which is better: wealth or free time? Why don't more people live as hunter-gatherers? Perhaps they can't, since they would need much more land.

Sahlins, Marshall (1974) 'The original affluent society', in *Stone Age Economics*, London: Tavistock Publications, pp. 1-39.

Scott, George C. (2017) *Against the Grain: A Deep History of the Earliest States*, New Haven: Yale University Press. A key part of his argument is on pages 150-82. There he argues that slavery, rather than crop domestication as such, was the cause of supposed 'advances'.

FILMS

There exist many films about hunter-gatherers. Let me just single out one for comment here, *Nanook of the North*, which is available on YouTube. It is silent, but with background music. It lasts just over an hour.

The film was made in 1922 and caused great controversy. Nevertheless it is a classic: it depicts life in the Canadian Arctic at that time. Why the controversy? Well, we must note that in 1922 what we today take for granted about the difference between documentary and drama simply didn't exist. For a start, Nanook wasn't the actor's real name, and he was not married to his screen wife: but the filmmaker was! Or at least that is what has been claimed. 'Nanook' knew about guns, but he was supposed to hunt a walrus as his ancestors did: with a spear. It proved impossible to film inside an igloo, so a three-sided one had to be constructed. Above all, the man who played Nanook did not die of starvation not long after the film was completed. (I was taught that in an anthropology class around 1970.) He survived, but later he did die of tuberculosis.

Among other films available on YouTube are:

- *Bushman: Once We Were Hunters* (Namibia)
- *The Life of an Il Torobo Hunter-Gatherer* (Kenya)
- *Hadzabe Hut Building* (Tanzania)
- *Fishing Trip with Pygmy Hunter-Gatherers* (Cameroun)
- *Dreamtime: Travelling through the Australian Continent* (Australia)
- *The Secret of Dreaming: An Australian Aboriginal Myth of Creation* (Australia)

… and, of course, many others. Some are partly fictional, but they all aim to provide a good picture of a hunter-gatherer way of life.

ACADEMIC JOURNALS

You would not be expected to read much academic literature. It can be dense stuff and difficult for many readers. However, if you are interested try these.

Hunter Gatherer Research
Established initially as *Before Farming*. The title seemed strange to some, so it was later changed to Hunter Gatherer Research. Published four times a year by Liverpool University Press. This the only academic journal dedicated exclusively to hunter-gatherer studies.

Nomadic Peoples
Many journals contain the odd article about hunter-gatherers, but *Nomadic Peoples* contains a good number. Most of the articles in the journal, though, are about herders.

Senri Ethnological Studies
Published by the National Museum of Ethnology in Osaka, Japan. Not really a journal but a publications series. Contains a great many articles on hunter-gatherers.

**Hearing
Others'
Voices**

Hearing Others' Voices is a transcultural and transdisciplinary book series in simple and straightforward language—to inform and engage general readers, undergraduates and, above all, sixth formers in recent advances in thought, unaccountably overlooked areas of the world, and key issues of the day.

www.ingramcontent.com/pod-product-compliance
Lightning Source LLC
Chambersburg PA
CBHW041216030426
42336CB00023B/3358